TRANSATLANTIC LINERS
In Picture Postcards

LOADING FREIGHT IN CUNARD STEAMERS AT LIVERPOOL DOCKS.

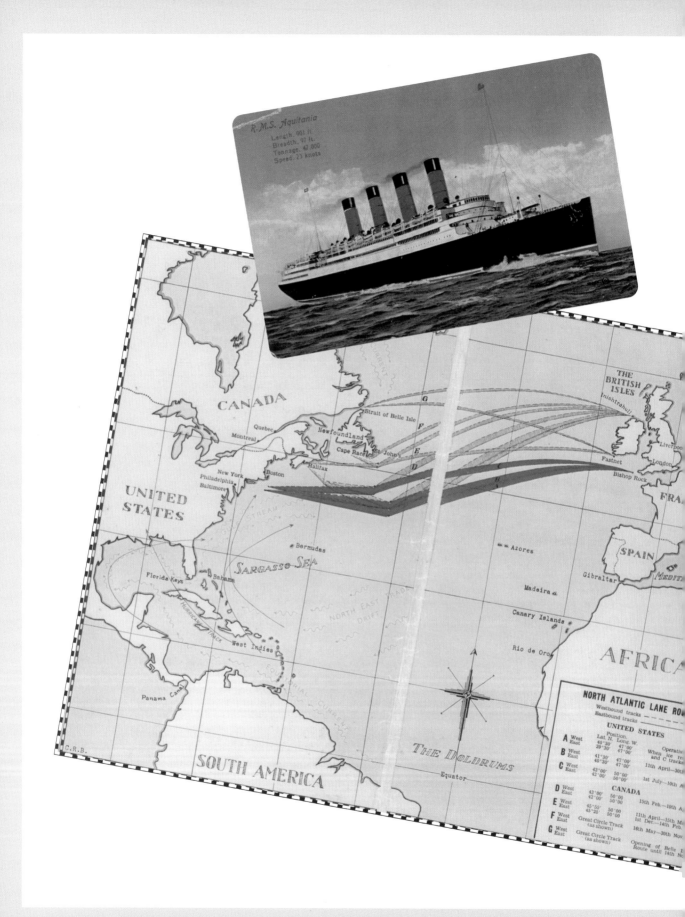

R.M.S. Aquitania

Length 901 ft.
Breadth, 97 ft.
Tonnage, 47,000
Speed, 23 knots

THE
BRITISH
ISLES

Inishtrahull

CANADA

Strait of Belle Isle

Quebec

Newfoundland

Montreal

St. John's

Cape Race

Liverpool

Fastnet

Halifax

London

Boston

Bishop Rock

New York

Philadelphia

Baltimore

UNITED
STATES

FRA

STREAM

GULF

Bermudas

Azores

SARGASSO SEA

SPAIN

Florida Keys

Bahama

Gibraltar

Madeira

MEDI

NORTH EAST TRADE

HURRICANE TRACK

Canary Islands

West Indies

Rio de Oro

Panama Canal

AFRICA

EQUATORIAL CURRENT

THE DOLDRUMS

SOUTH AMERICA

Equator

C.R.B.

NORTH ATLANTIC LANE RO

Westbound tracks
Eastbound tracks

UNITED STATES

		Position		
		Lat. N.	Long. W.	
A	West	40°30'	47°00'	Operativ
	East	39°30'	47°00'	When ice r
B	West	41°30'	47°00'	and C tracks
	East	40°30'	47°00'	
C	West	43°00'	50°00'	11th April—30t
	East	42°00'	50°00'	
				1st July—10th A

CANADA

D	West	43°00'	50°00'	
	East	42°00'	50°00'	15th Feb—10th A
E	West	45°55'	50°00'	
	East	45°20'	50°00'	11th April—15th M
F	West			1st Dec—14th Feb.
	East	Great Circle Track (as shown)		16th May—30th Nov
G	West	Great Circle Track (as shown)		Opening of Belle I
	East			Route until 14th N

TRANSATLANTIC LINERS
In Picture Postcards

Robert McDougall and

Robin Gardiner

Ian Allan
PUBLISHING

CONTENTS

FOREWORD
5

EVOLUTION OF THE LINERS
10

GOOD AND BAD TIMES
34

THE GOLDEN AGE
72

Half title page: Ivernia[1] (left), 1900, and Caronia[1] (1905) in Huskinson Dock, Liverpool, circa 1911. Ivernia would become a casualty of war in 1917.

Title page, top to bottom: Aquitania, a rare colour postcard of Cunard's most successful liner. North Atlantic route map. Extolling the virtues of Liverpool

First published 2004

ISBN 0 7110 3026 X

Published by Ian Allan Publishing

an imprint of Ian Allan Publishing Ltd, Hersham, Surrey KT12 4RG.
Printed in England by Ian Allan Printing Ltd, Hersham, Surrey KT12 4RG.

Code: 0410/B2

FOREWORD

The years when transatlantic liners truly reigned supreme spanned roughly a century from about 1870 until 1970, altogether a hundred years of incredible achievement by ship owners and builders that will never be forgotten.

The postcards and other illustrations in this book are from my private collection and give a broad representation of the way it was during the heyday of transatlantic voyaging. Many of the major transatlantic shipping lines of all nationalities are represented, along with most of the shipping companies that operated out of Britain from about 1900.

The two main passenger terminals in Britain during this golden age were Liverpool and Southampton, although others such as London and Bristol saw their fair share of transatlantic passengers. Liverpool's Mersey Docks & Harbour Company showed great foresight from the mid-1880s when it developed no fewer than seven miles of quays. Its main competitor, Southampton, rapidly developed to keep pace and, with the construction of the famous Ocean Dock in 1907, eventually became the more important terminal. The new deep water dock, with its purpose-built landing stages, railway terminal, ancillary shipping company facilities such as laundries and offices, and its proximity to London, had advantages that no other British port could ever compete with. Unlike Liverpool, with its complex arrangement of dock gates and smaller docks which slowed down the turn-around of large vessels, even the biggest of liners could easily enter and leave Southampton.

Although there was a rail terminal at Liverpool's Prince's Dock, the boat trains often terminated at Lime Street station, about a mile from the landing stage. This simple inconvenience to passengers burdened with luggage was yet another factor in the rise of Southampton as the premier British passenger port. In 1904, to make the Prince's landing stage more attractive to passengers and those seeing them off, the Mersey Dock managers, at the behest of the White Star and Cunard Lines, dredged the dock to give deeper water for ever-larger vessels. They built a 100yd-long pier, on 20ft-high foundations, to give unrestricted access to liners moored at the landing stage. A new open-fronted promenade, also built in 1904, gave a panoramic view of the River Mersey and the Prince's Landing Stage. Steel and wooden corridors were provided, leading directly to the embarkation and disembarkation points for moored liners from the huge passenger reception and customs hall.

Despite their best efforts the harbour managers were beset by problems, not the least being the four-knot river current that continually deposited

Right: An early view of Prince's Landing Stage at Liverpool with the Cunard Line's *Etruria*.

Right: In 1906 the new Ocean Dock was constructed at Southampton.

Below: Southampton's Ocean Dock was made deep enough to accommodate even the largest liners that were being planned. To the present day the world's largest liners still use the dock, even though a century has passed since it was planned.

Above right: Ocean Dock at Southampton in the 1950s, with Cunard's *Queen Elizabeth* berthed on the left.

Right: White Star's *Majestic*[2], formerly the Hamburg Amerika Line's *Bismarck* (1914). The world's largest liner is seen entering the world's largest dry-dock at Southampton in 1925

OCEAN DOCK, SOUTHAMPTON

sand in front of the landing stage. Dredging was a never-ending process and the accumulating sand made moorings unstable. As a consequence of this continual silting, liners often had to anchor in the middle of the River Mersey, and passengers, crew, supplies and fuel had to be ferried out by tender. Alternatively ships could negotiate the complex arrangement of lock gates to find a mooring but this was time-consuming and expensive. Given the problems that the Liverpool harbour management were faced with, it is hardly surprising that the port slowly deteriorated in importance as a liner terminal.

Southampton, on the other hand, from 1907 onwards offered better and better facilities for its transatlantic passengers. The new Ocean Dock, open to the River Test, could accommodate any size of ocean liner without the slightest difficulty. The railway terminal, actually on the dockside and at the same level, meant that passengers never had to carry luggage far or up a steep gradient, as they had to at Liverpool. Passengers could get on a train in London and get off again

R.M.S. "LAKE CHAMPLAIN."

LIVERPOOL LANDING STAGE.

Top: Liverpool's Prince's Landing
Stage, circa 1910, with the Cunard
liner *Campania*.

Above: Lake Champlain at
Liverpool's Prince's Landing Stage,
circa 1905, after she had transferred
to the Canadian Pacific Line.

alongside the ship they were to sail in
and the system worked equally we
the other way around for incomin
travellers. Prosperous passengers
their families, and well-wishers wh
arrived early at the Hampshir
port, could stay at the five-sta
South Western Hotel, whic
overlooked the Ocean Dock an
had its own rail link.

Unlike at Liverpool, whe
cargoes and luggage wer
stored in warehouses som
distance from the landin
stage, the Ocean Dock had it
own on-site facilities, even t
a massive laundry to dea
with soiled linen fron
arriving liners. Whil
Cunard continued to us
Liverpool as its main base o
operations, in 1907 White Star bega
to use Southampton for its first clas
express transatlantic liners sailing t
New York, although the ships wer
still registered at the company'
Liverpool headquarters. White Sta
continued to use Liverpool for it
less prestigious Atlantic services.

As the years passed, th
numbers of people wanting t
cross the Atlantic by shi
slowly declined and the majo
lines had to reduce fare
drastically to win a share o
what passenger traffic ther
was. Freight charges als
came down, so in order t
satisfy the demand fo
profits by shareholder
some of the lines
managements decided to resor
to sharp practices. White Star was at the forefron
of these rule-bending exercises and from about 1910 was doin
its best to secure an income from the maritime insurance
companies.

American shipping companies which were not affiliated to
J. P. Morgan's huge International Mercantile Marine organisation
which had swallowed up about a third of the transatlantic lines by
1902, began to canvass senators and Congress for an investigation
into the sharp practices of the White Star Line. According to these
American owners, the White Star Line not only flouted safety
regulations at sea but also imposed inhumane conditions on its lower
deck crews that amounted to near slavery.

Left: Cunard's paddle steamer *Persia* at Liverpool landing stage some time around 1903.

lines, and White Star in particular. On 27 March 1912 the White Star Line chairman, Joseph Bruce Ismay, wrote to Booth, Cunard Line chairman, notifying him that White Star's New York managers had succeeded in diverting the American investigation. However, a month later White Star was to become the subject of an official American inquiry following the *Titanic* disaster.

Transatlantic liners of today are little more than cruise ships. Cruising was pioneered by the White Star Line from the 1920s and early 30s and for a time the company practically cornered the market in this field. Unfortunately this was not good enough for the board of directors and to boost profits, to satisfy the demands of shareholders, several dubious practices were indulged in. Inevitably, the directors were eventually caught out and the line, by now under the direction of Lord Kylsant, was forced into liquidation. White Star was merged with Cunard in 1934, and although the majority of the White Star fleet was quickly disposed of, the last White Star transatlantic liner, *Britannic* [3], survived in service until 1960. Cunard continues to cross the Atlantic with large passenger ships, having recently brought the new *Queen Mary 2* into service.*

The Cunard Line, in 1902, under its chairman Mr A. Booth, based at the company's Liverpool headquarters, was aware of the White Star Line's questionable mode of management. However, Booth had personal relationships with White Star's directors and they were all members of the same Masonic lodges, so, without actually aiding and abetting, he turned a blind eye to their covert insurance scams.

Both Cunard and White Star were worried about the impending March 1912 investigation by America into the major British shipping

Robert McDougall
April 2004

*For further information on the White Star Line and the *Titanic* story, the following titles from Ian Allan Publishing may be of interest:

The History of the White Star Line, ISBN 0 7110 2809 5

White Star Line in Picture Postcards, ISBN 0 7110 2986 5

Titanic: the Ship That Never Sank, ISBN 0 7110 2777 3

Titanic in Picture Postcards, ISBN 0 7110 2896 6

Who Sailed on Titanic: The Definitive Passenger Lists, ISBN 0 7110 2880 X

Left: Author Robert McDougall at Liverpool's docks.

EVOLUTION OF THE LINERS

The era of the passenger liner was ushered in by the harnessing of steam power in such a way that it could be used efficiently to propel a ship through the water. With the benefit of hindsight this does not appear to be too much of a problem, but the pioneers did not have the benefit of hindsight. What they did was being done for the first time.

The first practical steam engine appears to have been made some time shortly before 1663 by the English Marquis of Worcester. His engine, like most of those that followed closely behind, was primarily intended to pump water out of mines. The marquis's invention was largely ignored until some 30 years later when Thomas Savery saw its potential. Savery refined the marquis's machine until, in 1689, he produced his own machine, a beam engine. This engine relied on the rapid condensation of steam in its cylinder to produce a vacuum which sucked the piston up. By 1712 Thomas Newcomen had refined Savery's engine further and fitted it with a pump, still with the clearing of water from mines as its primary function. Newcomen's engine, like those of the Marquis of Worcester and Thomas Savery, still relied on the condensation of steam to produce its power, so producing steam at any more than atmospheric pressure was unnecessary. Newcomen's engine, though a big improvement on anything that had come before, was still very large and produced very little power for its size. Nevertheless, it was

these low-powered steam condensation engines that opened the way for the production of the first steamers. In 1736 an English inventor called Jonathan Hull fitted a miniature Newcomen engine driving a stern-mounted paddle wheel, driven by belts, into a boat. Hull's small vessel, the first steam-powered tugboat, showed the way but there was still a long way to go.

In 1769 a Scottish engineer, James Watt, patented a new kind of steam engine in which the piston was driven along the cylinder by steam at more than atmospheric pressure. For the first time an engine was available that could produce a decent amount of power for its size. It was not long before the double-acting steam engine came on the scene. This engine with its piston driven along the cylinder in both directions automatically doubled the machine's potential power output.

In 1783 a Frenchman, the Marquis Claude François de Jouffroy d'Abbans, built a paddle steamer, displacing 182 tons and almost 100ft long. Though not commercially viable, the *Pyrosaphe*, using a double-acting engine, did sail up the Saône near Lyon for a quarter of an hour and so must be considered successful.

Not everyone thought that the way forward was with the use of paddle wheels. John Fitch, a Connecticut watchmaker, and Johann Voigt, produced an oddity in 1787 which was driven through the water by six oars on either side of the vessel, powered by one of

Left: The first transatlantic liner Isambard Kingdom Brunel's *Great Western* on her maiden voyage in 1838.

Right: Samuel Cunard, founder of the Cunard Line.

mes Watt's engines. The peculiar contraption did manage to achieve a speed of 8 knots on the Delaware River. None of these early steamers was capable of going to sea and a lot of technical improvement was necessary before they could become practical working vessels. Those improvements were not long in coming and the beginning of the 19th century saw huge steps forward.

In 1802 the *Charlotte Dundas*, built by William Symington, successfully towed two 70-ton barges along the Forth and Clyde Canal for a distance of 19 miles in 6 hours. Then, in 1807, Robert Fulton's *Clermont*, another side-paddle steamer, began the first regular passenger service between New York and Albany. This elegant, purpose-built, 100-ton vessel was the very first to supply a commercial passenger service using steam, although still not at sea. Another three decades would pass before the first ocean-going steamships became practical.

The age of the transatlantic liner can be divided into three periods. The first period, from about 1838 to 1903, covered the transition from sail to steam propulsion and the change in ship design from clippers to what we would today recognise as a passenger vessel. The second period was the start of the heyday of the liners with the great shipping companies such as Cunard, Allan, Inman, Canadian Pacific, Royal Mail, White Star, Norddeutscher (North German) Lloyd and Hamburg Amerika, and many lesser players such as the French and Italian lines. The third period saw new classic liners entering into service, but also witnessed the decline in seaborne passenger traffic across the Atlantic after World War 2 to the present day as aircraft came of age and the last of the liners became nothing more than cruise ships.

The transatlantic liner age really began on 8 April 1838 when the Great Western Railway Company's *Great Western* left Bristol for New York. The Great Western Steamship Company had been formed in June 1836 under the direction of Marc Brunel, father of Isambard Kingdom Brunel and was based at Bristol. Their *Great Western*, designed by Isambard Brunel and launched in July 1837 before an audience of 50,000 people, was the first purpose-built transatlantic liner. Before then other steam vessels had made the passage from the Old World to the New but always mainly under sail. However, just four days before the *Great Western* left Bristol, the British & American Steam Navigation Company's paddle steamer *Sirius* had departed from Cork, also for New York, in an effort to make the crossing primarily under steam power.

The 703-ton *Sirius* had never been intended as a transatlantic vessel at all but had been rented by the British & American Company to establish a regular steam service between England and Ireland. The company had, in 1835, ordered a special ship of 1,968 tons from a Clyde shipyard with which to set up the regular transatlantic passenger service but because of a delay with the

engines the vessel was not ready in time. The little paddle steamer *Sirius* would have to do the job as best she could.

Sirius, loaded down with passengers, mail, cargo and 400 tons of coal set off on 4 April 1838. With her 320-horsepower engines she managed to make an average speed of 6 ½ knots and arrived at New York on 22 April after a passage lasting 18 days and 10 hours. Just 12 hours later the *Great Western* arrived with 111 passengers on board.

The *Great Western*, like *Sirius*, was a paddle steamer but there the similarity ended. At 1,319 tons and 212ft long she was almost twice the size, and with her two engines putting out 750 horsepower she was considerably faster. Designed by Isambard Kingdom Brunel, for the Great Western Steamship Company, as an express passenger ship, the *Great Western* had made the crossing in just 15 days and 5 hours at an average speed of 8 ¾ knots. Within the space of one day the two ships had changed the world. *Sirius* had made the first Atlantic crossing under steam power and *Great Western* had become the first transatlantic passenger liner.

Great Western served the Great Western Steamship Company for only eight years before she was sold to the Royal Mail Steam Packet Company who mainly provided a steamship service to the West Indies. The liner was requisitioned by the British Government for use as a troopship during the Crimean War. In 1857 she was scrapped at Castle's yard on the River Thames.

Samuel Cunard, the founder of the longest-lived transatlantic shipping line of them all, was born on 21 November 1787 at Halifax, Nova Scotia, the second son of Abraham Cunard. The Cunards, who were Quakers, had emigrated from Redditch in the Midlands to Philadelphia in the 17th century. Although the family lived in America, they still considered themselves to be British so when the American War of Independence broke out they moved to Nova Scotia.

By 1813 Abraham Cunard & Son had become a prominent business operating sailing ships, an ironworks and a whale fishery. This same year the company despatched its first transatlantic vessel, *White Oak*. Samuel's brothers all engaged in a seafaring life, mostly between Nova Scotia and the West Indies. Young Samuel was also interested in the sea and shipping, but not as a sailor. Samuel Cunard's interest lay in owning and operating his own ships. When Samuel was only 27 years of age Cunard & Son took on the contract to convey British mails between Halifax, Newfoundland, Boston and Bermuda. This contract was carried out to the complete satisfaction of the British Government by sailing vessels operating at Cunard's own financial risk. Also in 1814 Samuel Cunard married Susan Duffus, daughter of John Duffus, a prominent Halifax business man. The union was blessed with two sons and seven daughters.

In 1819 Abraham Cunard retired and the company was renamed Samuel Cunard & Co. By the time Samuel Cunard was 40 he was estimated to be worth more than $200,000 — an enormous sum at that time. In 1825, during a visit to England, Samuel became an agent for the Honourable East India Company. As a result of this agency, the East India Company began to ship its tea for the area through Halifax, to the great financial benefit of Halifax in general and Samuel Cunard in particular.

Despite his association with sailing vessels, Cunard firmly believed that the future lay in steam. He held that there was no reason why steam-driven ships, properly designed, built and manned, should not sail from one point to another with the punctuality of railway trains. The idea of an ocean railway was one of his favourites, and it was an idea he would make a reality. His first move in that direction could be said to be his involvement with the *Royal William*. At the top of the list of 144 subscribers who g together to build that steamship is the name of Samuel Cunard.

The *Royal William*, built at Quebec, was launched in 183 The original intention was that the ship would run between Queb and Pictou in Nova Scotia but for financial reasons this route w changed. The new route chosen was between Pictou and Londo The *Royal William* completed her voyage, arriving at the Isle Wight in just 17 days, confirming the practicality of transatlan steam navigation, although that was not the purpose of the journe The *Royal William* had been sent across the Atlantic to where s could be sold for the best price.

During the period between 1833 and 1838 Samuel Cuna continued to distribute the British mails to their destinations Canada, the United States, Newfoundland and Bermuda. S successful was he that by this time he had no fewer than 40 vesse

Left: Samuel Cunard's first transatlantic mail steamer *Britannia* leaving Liverpool at the start of her maiden voyage on 4 July 1840.

Below left: Brunel's *Great Britain*, the first iron-hulled screw-driven liner, at Bristol in 1843.

Top right: The Collins Line's *Arctic*, which foundered in 1854 after a collision with a small French vessel. Among the 322 lost were the founder of the line's wife, son and daughter.

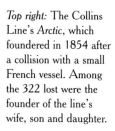

OGDEN'S CIGARETTES.

THE "ARCTIC."

ader his control. All the time he watched the
ady development of the steamships that
ere beginning to replace the old sailing
ips. Then, in 1838, came his opportunity.

As a result of the successful crossing of
e Atlantic by the *Great Western* and *Sirius*
ader steam power alone, the Lords
ommissioners of the Admiralty issued a
rcular asking for tenders for a steam
acket company to carry Her Majesty's
ails on the Atlantic. Not a single
itish steamship owner responded.

The British Government was on
e verge of abandoning the project
hen Samuel Cunard, who had heard of the
rcular, arrived in Britain. Cunard had been delayed by his
nsuccessful attempts to find financial assistance in Halifax. He had
clear idea of where to find the financial aid he sought in Britain
at he had been given a letter of introduction to the Clyde
ipbuilder Robert Napier by James Melville, Secretary of the
onourable East India Company. Napier introduced him to two
her shipowners, George Burns and David MacIver. After two
ays of talks Burns and MacIver agreed to the formation of a new
eamship line. The necessary capital of £270,000 was quickly
ised and an offer made for the conveyance of Her Majesty's Mails
very fortnight between Liverpool, Halifax and Boston. In response
the request for tenders, Cunard proposed to supply three new
eamers of about 800 tons and 300 horsepower each for a
uaranteed subsidy of £55,000 a year, an enormous sum in those
ays. The government agreed and a seven year contract was signed.

Cunard now had the contract but he did not have the ships he
eeded. Advice was requested from William Kidston & Sons of
lasgow as to which would be the best shipyard to build the new
essels at the budgeted cost of £90,000. The famous Clyde
ipbuilding firm of Robert Napier wanted £96,000 to construct
e three ships Cunard needed but agreed to the offered £30,000
piece when Cunard explained that the vessels were to be identical.
he new ships were to be wooden-hulled paddle steamers of slightly
ore than 1,000 tons apiece and capable of 9 knots. Within six
onths a fourth ship was added to the order. Those first four ships
ere the *Britannia*, *Acadia*, *Caledonia* and *Columbia*.

On arrival at Halifax the mail would travel overland to Pictou
n the St Lawrence, and from there by ship to Quebec. Cunard
ould need another small steamer for the last part of that journey,
he bought the Liverpool to Glasgow coastal packet *Unicorn* from
. & J. Burns and sailed aboard her for Halifax.

The first vessel, *Britannia*, 1,154 tons, 207ft in length and with
ccommodation for 115 cabin passengers, arrived in Halifax during
e night of 16/17 July 1840. *Britannia* had left Liverpool on 4 July
ith her first consignment of mail and had made the inaugural
rossing in 12 days, and reached Boston in just two more. She
ould remain with the company until 1849, sailing between
iverpool, Halifax and Boston.

As Charles Dickens noted when he crossed the Atlantic aboard

Britannia in 1842, these mail ships were
anything but comfortable. They were small, quarters were cramped
and the ships' engines caused continuous vibration, but they were
faster and more reliable than sailing ships. Nevertheless, Dickens
made his return voyage under sail.

In April 1843 the *Hibernia* entered Cunard service as a reserve
ship in case any of the initial four were unable to fulfil their part of
the contract. She had arrived none too soon as the *Columbia* ran
aground between Boston and Halifax. All of the people aboard, 85
of them passengers, were saved but the ship was lost.

Columbia's permanent replacement, *Cambria*, joined the line in
January 1845.

The *Great Britain*, another of Brunel's designs for the Great
Western Steamship Company although not quite so successful as his
first, was launched in 1843, six years after construction had begun.
Although not completely profitable, the *Great Britain* was a
landmark ship inasmuch as she had a hull built of iron and was
driven by a screw propeller. The first Atlantic crossing was made in
1845 but at nothing like the expected speed. Unfortunately a blade
came off the six-bladed propeller and the engines did not develop as
much power as anticipated; eventually the voyage was completed
under sail alone. In September 1846 *Great Britain* ran aground off
the Irish coast. Demonstrating just how strong Brunel's iron hull
was, *Great Britain* remained stranded for 11 months before being
refloated and transferred to the Australian route. The ship seemed
to have come to the end of the line when she became a coal hulk and
was run aground on the Falkland Islands. However, despite the
battering she received over the years from South Atlantic storms, the
ship was finally brought back to England in 1970 and completely
restored. Today she serves as a nautical museum at Bristol, where
she was built more than a century earlier. Iron hulls were obviously
capable of withstanding the worst that the Atlantic could throw at
them.

In 1846 Cunard's mail contract came up for renewal and some
members of the British parliament favoured awarding the contract to
the Great Western Steamship Company but it refused to guarantee

regular sailings during the winter months from November to April. Cunard, on the other hand, promised an all year round service, weekly in the summer time and fortnightly during the winter, and to equip his vessels as transports for use by the British armed services in time of war. Cunard again won his contract. A new delivery point was also agreed upon, New York. The extra distance meant that Cunard would need more ships to maintain his schedule so four were ordered. The *America* started her maiden voyage on 15 April 1848, followed by *Niagara* on 20 May, *Europa* on 15 July and *Canada* on 25 November.

The Cunard Line did have its disasters, just like any other enterprise, and in 1849 its paddle steamer *Europa* ran down the brig *Charles Bartlett* in the River Mersey. The brig quickly foundered with the loss of 134 lives.

During the first 10 years of its existence the Cunard Line had enjoyed an almost complete monopoly of the North Atlantic steamer trade. Its only real rival was the Collins Line which tried to win business by providing faster and more luxurious vessels. Edward Knight Collins had taken exception to Cunard's domination of the North Atlantic. The American Government agreed with him so Collins, already a very successful sailing ship owner, decided in 1846 to sell them all and go into steam. It was his intention, with government backing, to build the finest, largest and fastest ships for the Atlantic. He also wanted to build his new ships out of iron but American shipyards were not up to the task so he had to settle for wooden-hulled paddle steamers of about 2,800 tons, but capable of better than 12 knots. The first four ships were named *Atlantic*, *Pacific*, *Arctic* and *Baltic*, and were all bigger and faster than anything in the Cunard fleet.

In 1851, during the Great Exhibition in London, the *Baltic* managed to cross the Atlantic in 9 days and 10 hours, and so became the holder of a purely notional honour 'The Blue Riband of the Atlantic' for the fastest crossing. The Blue Riband became a reality in 1935 when a silver trophy about four feet high and weighing in at between 25 and 30lb was donated by Henry Pidduck & Sons, silversmiths, of Hanley. The trophy was designed by Mr Charles Holliday and symbolised the evolution of the modern liner. At its base are seated figures of Neptune and Amphitrite. Rising above them, supporting the Blue Riband, are figures of Victory. Above them is a large globe, surmounted by figures symbolising speed overcoming the power of the Atlantic.

The Collins Line ships were a commercial disaster, even though they were popular with the travelling public. Although the ships in their first 28 round trips carried half as many people again as Cunard's vessels, they showed a loss of $2.5 million. MacIver, one of Cunard's partners, wrote to him about the challenge from Collins: 'The Collins people are pretty much in the situation of finding that breaking our windows with sovereigns, though very fine fun, is too costly to keep up.' MacIver was absolutely correct.

Then, in 1854, in thick fog some 60 miles from Cape Race, the *Arctic* was rammed by a small French vessel. Captain Luce of the *Arctic* tried to reach land but his vessel sank after about 20 miles. The crew, with the notable exception of Captain Luce, took to the boats and abandoned the passengers to their fate, among them

Collins' own wife, son and daughter. Only about a quarter of t[he] 365 people aboard were saved.

In 1855 Collins launched an even larger ship, the 4,114-t[on] *Adriatic*. But a year later disaster struck again when the *Paci[fic]* disappeared without trace. The US Government withdrew [its] subsidy and Collins was forced to sell off the rest of his fleet to p[ay] his creditors. The Collins Line had failed but not before it ha[d] established that wooden-hulled steamers were not strong enough f[or] the North Atlantic trade, that American-built ships with America[n] crews were too expensive (American sailors were paid approximate[ly] double the wages of their British counterparts), and that bigger w[as] better. Collins' ships had been larger, more opulent and faster th[an] their Cunard rivals. Where Cunard vessels had tiny, sparse passeng[er] cabins heated by a small stove, Collins' liners had steam heating a[nd] carpets; no wonder the public had preferred them.

In response to the Collins challenge Cunard had ordered tw[o] new ships, both to be bigger and more opulent than the Colli[ns] vessels, the *Arabia* and *Persia*. *Arabia* was sold before she w[as] completed to the Royal Mail Line to replace its *Amazon*, which ha[d] burned out. *Persia* became *Arabia*[2] and was soon joined by the *Al[ps]* and *Andes*.

In 1853 an investigative journalist who was looking in[to] conditions aboard British emigrant ships at Liverpool found them [to] be in an appalling state. Lifeboats were so rotten that they wou[ld] have been useless in an emergency even if they could have bee[n] loaded and lowered, which would have been impossible becau[se] they were being used as extra bunkers.

The Allan Line was in existence from 1854 until 1917 (b[ut] ceased to be a true shipping line a year earlier when the vast majori[ty] of its fleet was taken over by the Canadian Pacific Line.) Un[til] February 1883 the line's British activities had been pretty mu[ch] confined to Liverpool, Glasgow and Moville in Ireland. Then t[he] Allan Line became the London agent of the newly formed Tw[in] Screw Line, which operated between London and New York, an[d] in no time it had made enough contacts in the British capital to s[et] up its own service between London and Canada.

In 1850 William Inman, who had no interest whatsoever in t[he] Atlantic first class trade but only in immigrant traffic, just happene[d] to see the new 1,600-ton Clyde-built steamer *City of Glasgow*. H[e] was impressed. Until then Inman had run the Richardson Line [of] sailing packets which carried emigrants from Liverpool [to] Philadelphia. Business had been going downhill for some tim[e] because most emigrants preferred to go to New York, and to travel o[n] the newer and larger American vessels engaged in the same trade. H[e] persuaded the Richardson brothers to buy the *City of Glasgow* an[d] she made her first voyage for the Richardsons on 17 December 185[0] still on the Philadelphia route, with 400 emigrant passengers aboar[d.] She was an immediate success. The *City of Glasgow* was the fir[st] screw-driven ship regularly to carry steerage passengers to Americ[a.] The *City of Glasgow* disappeared in April 1854 while on an Atlant[ic] passage, with 430 people aboard. Inmans believed that the ship ha[d] run into ice and had foundered. Two other passenger packets were lo[st] in 1854. These were the Pennsylvania Steamship Company's *City [of] Philadelphia* and the previously mentioned Collins Line's *Arctic.*

Had it been left to Inman, conditions aboard the *City of Glasgow* would have been at least as bad, if not worse, for the migrants than they had been aboard his sailing ships. He wanted to pack as many as 1,000 people into the ship but government regulations limited the number to 600. In the middle of the 19th century conditions for the poor in Europe were particularly harsh, vast numbers were making their way to America and the promise of a new life. And quite a few were coming back, having discovered that this new life was not all it was cracked up to be. Just by cutting the time a passage to America took, by as much as half, life was made far less unpleasant for the average emigrant. Added to that, Inman fed his passengers well, not for any altruistic reasons but to ensure that they were in good enough condition to pass inspection by American immigration officials on their arrival. There was no profit in having to bring would-be emigrants back home because the Americans did not want them. This inspection by immigration officers in America, although feared by immigrants, was actually of great benefit to them. Gone were the days when starving and diseased people could be herded aboard a ship like cattle, and transported across the Atlantic. However, the same could not be said for those on the Australian route, but that is outside the scope of this book.

Inman's next vessel was the iron-hulled *City of Brussels*, which was also a screw-driven ship. Propellers were in their infancy and ships equipped with them were generally a little slower than paddle steamers although still faster than sailing ships. This did not matter to Inman's emigrant passengers as they were in no particular hurry – most were being fed, watered and accommodated better than they had ever been in their lives before.

As things turned out, the properly designed propeller was much more efficient than the paddle wheel as trials between the *Rattler* and *Alecto* in 1845 had conclusively proved. The British Admiralty had arranged a tug of war between two ships of equal displacement and horsepower. The *Alecto* was driven by paddles and the *Rattler* by propeller. With both vessels running at full power the *Rattler* towed *Alecto* backwards at 2 ½ knots. So it should have come as no surprise to Inman when his screw-driven ship *City of Paris* took the Blue Riband in 1866. By that time, the immigration trade having dropped off a little, Inman was carrying first and second class passengers along with steerage. He was in direct competition with Samuel Cunard but while Inmans had lost no fewer than five vessels in 30 years, two of them with considerable loss of life, Cunard had not lost any.

Inman himself died in 1881, just a few days after the launching of what was intended to be his greatest ship, the *City of Rome*. It was probably just as well that Inman did not survive to see his vessel's somewhat less than illustrious career. Quite probably the best looking liner ever built, and meant to be one of the fastest at 18 ½, knots the 8,400-ton vessel never lived up to expectation. This, the first three-funnel ship, never made an Atlantic crossing in less than 10 days and after just six round voyages was returned to the builders. From there she was sold on to various owners and eventually sank at her berth while being scrapped.

The Donaldson Line was founded in 1855 and survived until 1966. In the early years, from about 1876, the line was occupied in transporting Scottish migrants to Canada. From 1905 first and second class passengers were also carried. For much of its life the Donaldson Line worked with the Anchor Line with the combination being commonly known as Anchor Donaldson. The Anchor Line itself had been founded in 1856, survived for 110

years and was wound up in 1966. T[...]
Caledonia, the Anchor Line's last sh[...]
which it had acquired in 1948, outliv[...]
the line until 1971.

The Guion Line was a dir[...]
descendant of the Black Star Line [...]
sailing packets, and a more disreputa[...]
shipping line is difficult to imagi[...]
Black Star owned the very best a[...]
largest clippers sailing the No[...]
Atlantic. However, it crewed the[...]
vessels with the dregs of humanity fr[...]
New York bars and dockside dives. A[...]
consequence the line soon acquired [...]
unenviable reputation for defrauding a[...]
beating emigrant passengers. T[...]
company was run by the firm of Willia[...]
& Guion, and when the emigrant tra[...]
started to fall off in the 1850s and 60[...]
moved into steam. The line's name w[...]
changed to the Guion Line and it boug[...]
British-built steamers to operate out [...]
Liverpool.

In 1856 Cunard took delivery of [...]
first iron-hulled ship, *Persia*[2]. Not on[...]
was the new vessel fast — she took t[...]
Blue Riband with an Atlantic crossing [...]
13 ½ knots, completing the voyage [...]
nine days, four hours and 45 minutes[...]
but she also boasted the fine[...]
accommodation to be had on the Nor[...]
Atlantic.

By far the most famous of Brune[...]
ships was the *Great Eastern*, built for t[...]
Eastern Navigation Company. At alm[...]
700ft long and 18,914 tons the *Gr[...]
Eastern* was too big and too far advanc[...]
for the technology of her time. The tri[...]
and tribulations of building a[...]
launching the giant ship proved too mu[...]
for Isambard Kingdom Brunel and [...]

Top: Cunard's *Russia*
(1867), which took the Blue
Riband from *Scotia* during
her first year in service.

Above: Oceanic[1] (1871), the
first White Star Line liner,
and the first liner designed
and built as such. All the
liners that followed *Oceanic*
owed their looks to Edward
Harland's radical ship.

died on 15 September 1859, just a few months before his greate[...]
ship began her North Atlantic career. Between 1860 and 1863 t[...]
Great Eastern made nine Atlantic crossings but never recouped t[...]
cost of building her. On her maiden voyage the ship, thoug[...]
designed to accommodate 5,000 passengers, had only 36 aboa[...]
one of them Jules Verne. On a crossing in 1862 the *Great Easte*[...]
struck an uncharted rock off Montauk Point that ripped a hole 8[...]
by 9ft in her bottom. Brunel had designed the ship with a doub[...]
bottom and longitudinal and transverse bulkheads to withstand su[...]
damage, and she steamed into New York with only a slight li[...]
Eventually the vessel found a degree of success by laying the fi[...]
transatlantic telephone cable between Great Britain and the USA[...]
The huge size of the ship was not exceeded for 40 years until t[...]

hite Star Line's *Oceanic*[2] and her tonnage by the same mpany's *Baltic*[2] five years later.

During the Crimean and Boer Wars the Cunard Line stood by promise to the British Government to supply transports. Eleven unard vessels served the government during the Crimean conflict. efficiently did the line operate on the British behalf that in 1859 ueen Victoria conferred a baronetcy on Samuel Cunard. In 1862 e Cunard Line's first propeller-driven vessel, *China*, was delivered Robert Napier. The same builder also delivered the *Scotia*, the stest paddle steamer afloat, which would also have been the largest it for Brunel's *Great Eastern*. By this time the American Civil War as in full swing, so there was a drop in transatlantic business. Not ng before the war ended Samuel Cunard died at the ripe old age 78 on 20 April 1865.

The concern eventually best known as the Furness Withy Line as founded in 1865 as George Warren & Company, then became e Furness Warren Line and only adopted the Furness Withy title 1912. Furness Withy operated on the Liverpool, Boston and hiladelphia route until passenger services were abandoned in 961. In its final years it also took over what had been the Pacific team Navigation Company, which was actually formed in 1868 for e transatlantic trade. Pacific Steam Navigation was bought out by e Royal Mail Line in 1938 but was subsequently sold on to the urness Withy group.

The end of the American Civil War in 1865 brought a sharp crease in the number of people wishing to emigrate to America, so unard was obliged to increase its fleet. The first new ship was the va. In 1867 the *Russia* and *Siberia* joined the line, followed in 868 by the *Samaria* and the *Abyssinia*, and *Algeria* in 1870. owever, Cunard was not to have it all its own way for much longer.

The White Star Line was founded in 1845 by Henry Wilson d John Pilkington of Liverpool. After several changes of anagement and an over-ambitious programme of expansion and ip purchasing, the line was forced into liquidation in 1869. lmost immediately, for the princely sum of £1,000, the line's ame, house flag and what goodwill remained, was bought by homas Henry Ismay. With the assistance of Gustave Schwabe, a iverpool financier, Ismay set up the Oceanic Steam Navigation ompany with offices at Liverpool. Despite its rather grandiose fficial title, the company was universally known as the White Star ine and the house flag, a five-pointed white star in a red burgee, nsured the continuation of the name. Ismay promptly ordered four ew steamers from the Belfast shipbuilders, Harland & Wolff: ceanic, *Atlantic*, *Baltic* and *Republic*. Coincidentally, the Wolff de of the shipbuilder's partnership was Schwabe's nephew Gustav, a fair percentage of the money he put up would remain in the mily. No other shipbuilder would design and build ships for the Vhite Star Line, although the company would occasionally buy ips designed for, or used by, other lines.

Most of the contracts between White Star and Harland & Wolff ere on a 'cost plus profit' basis. In return for this guaranteed profit rrangement Harland & Wolff undertook not to build ships for Vhite Star's competitors. This arrangement, of course, made the o companies so interdependent that they were effectively one, but both companies did well out of the arrangement. Harland & Wolff built more than 50 ships for White Star, whilst the shipping line could always get a replacement when one of its vessels met with catastrophe — a quite regular occurrence.

Edward Harland had a few ideas of his own about how a passenger liner should be laid out. Until then passenger ships were just the same as cargo vessels but with a few deck houses added on to form the passenger accommodation. Harland's new ships would be designed from the bottom up with passenger accommodation in mind. Instead of the usual deck houses, the sides of the hull would be continued upwards to form the now familiar superstructure containing much of the passenger space, with covered promenade areas. First class passenger quarters were situated around the middle of the ships, and cabins and public rooms were much larger than those aboard vessels of any other line. Edward Harland's new ships were the very first modern liners, recognisable as such.

In 1871 Cunard faced its greatest challenge to date with the arrival on the North Atlantic of Thomas Ismay's White Star Line vessels. The White Star ships were successful and Ismay began to build a reputation for providing the most comfortable, if not the fastest, liners operating on the Atlantic. These ships were the first to be described as having all the comforts of first class Swiss hotels. The White Star Line also treated emigrant passengers far better than any other line, with the result that many people of all classes preferred to sail on its ships. Although Cunard commissioned two new ships in 1874, *Bothnia* and *Scythia*, these were still not up to the standards set by White Star.

The bad luck which would dog White Star throughout its long existence began in 1871 when its company name ship, *Oceanic*, developed serious engine trouble at the start of its maiden voyage and was forced to return to Liverpool for repairs.

By the end of 1871 two more ships, *Atlantic* and *Baltic*, had joined *Oceanic* on the White Star route between Liverpool and New York. However, despite being probably the finest vessels then operating on the North Atlantic, they managed to capture only a relatively small percentage of the market. Regular transatlantic travellers tended to remain loyal to the ships they were familiar with and had travelled on before.

In an effort to supplement the line's earnings and exploit the recent opening of the Suez Canal two more ships already under construction by Thomas Royden of Liverpool, the *Asiatic* and *Tropic*, were bought in 1871. Although originally intended for service to India, both of these ships would become transatlantic liners before long.

The following year, 1872, the fourth of Ismay's new ships, *Republic*, entered service on the Atlantic run, completing the line's initial order for vessels. White Star's intention was to operate a weekly transatlantic service and it was quickly calculated that to do this at least five ships would be required, and one in reserve would not hurt. It was considerably cheaper to have ships built by Harland & Wolff in pairs or more, so White Star ordered two more. These ships, *Adriatic* and *Celtic*, were slightly larger, improved, versions of the line's original four vessels, and they came into service in 1872. The spare ship, *Republic*, was put to work on the route between

Liverpool and Valparaiso, via Cape Horn, along with *Asiatic* and *Tropic* which had proved something of a disappointment on the Indian run. Two more new ships, *Gaelic* and *Belgic*, were purchased by White Star in 1873 for the Valparaiso route. Fortune appeared to be smiling on the line, then disaster struck.

The *Atlantic* ran into appalling weather conditions while making a westbound crossing. The ferocity of the wind and sea slowed the ship down despite the best efforts of her engineers and firemen. Fearing that they would run out of coal before reaching New York, Captain James Agnew Williams decided to make for Halifax, Nova Scotia. A series of minor mistakes in estimating the ship's course and speed led to her being about 12 or 13 miles from where her officers thought she was when she crashed into Marr's Rock. Immediately the heavy seas began to tear the stricken vessel apart. Of the 978 believed to be aboard, almost 200 children and up to 300 women among them, only 432 survived. None of the women and only one child was saved from the wreck. White Star now held a rather dubious record, that for the worst shipping disaster in history. Records, like pie crusts, are made to be broken and given time the White Star Line would break this one with the most famous maritime disaster ever.

In the meantime other lines had, of course, come into being but they contributed little to the development of the liner. The French Line established a reputation for serving the best food to be had on an Atlantic liner, as would be expected. The German lines, the Hamburg and North German Lloyd, had most of their ships built in Britain, and dealt almost exclusively in emigrant traffic. Given time, all that would change and the German and French lines would challenge the big two, Cunard and White Star, for supremacy on the Atlantic. Many other smaller lines would also appear and claim their share of the lucrative trade.

Among these challengers for the Atlantic passenger trade were the Allan Line, Red Star Line, American Line, Anchor, Netherlands, National, Inman, Leyland, Dominion, Canadian Pacific, and many other smaller competitors. However, for the golden years of the Atlantic liners the big names were Cunard, White Star, Canadian Pacific, Hamburg Amerika, and North German Lloyd.

White Star's South American service was discontinued in 1874 because profits were not up to the levels demanded by the company and two of the four vessels employed on it, *Asiatic* and *Tropic*, were sold off. The other two, *Gaelic* and *Belgic*, were put on to a cargo-only service between New York and London.

Two more sister ships had been ordered from Harland & Wolff: *Britannic* and *Germanic*. The first of these vessels, *Britannic*, specially designed to compete in speed with the best of the Cunard

ships operating on the North Atlantic, joined the line in 1874. H[er] sister would begin service the next year. In 1876, first the *Britann[ic]* and then *Germanic* managed to take the Blue Riband with averag[e] speeds of 15.4 and 15.8 knots respectively.

The next year brought an unlikely alliance. The North Atlant[ic] mail contract was shared between White Star, Inmans and Cunar[d] for the first time.

The Orient Line began in the 1820, and operated sailing ship[s] for the next half century but in 1878 it went over to steamers. Th[e] line continued until 1960 when it was merged with P&O (as th[e] famous Peninsular & Oriental Steam Navigatio[n] Company was usually known). The name P&[O] Orient Line remained in use until 1961 when [it] became just the P&O Line. In 1960, at the time [of] the merger between P&O and the Orient Line th[e] company had the largest fleet of liners then [in] existence. P&O Line, as the full version of i[ts] name suggests, was primarily occupied with th[e] Indian and Far East trade and was not really [a] transatlantic line at all (and therefore is n[ot] covered in detail here). However, on occasio[n] its vessels did cross the Atlantic and in mo[re] modern times its most famous shi[p] *Canberra*, did so regularly. *Canberra* saile[d] on her maiden voyage on 15 March 196[1] and operated as the line's flagship, sailin[g] all over the world, and as a troopshi[p] during the Falklands War, until h[er] recent retirement.

In 1879 the Guion Line steame[r] *Arizona* ran full tilt into an iceberg a[t] about 15 knots. The ship survived b[ut] with some 25ft of her bow crumpled up like [a] concertina. In 1877 and 1880 the company managed to wrec[k] two vessels within a couple of miles of one another near Anglese[y]. Then things suddenly improved and the *Alaska* snatched the Blu[e] Riband by crossing the Atlantic in less than a week at 16½ knot[s]. Guion then took delivery of an even faster vessel, the *Orego[n]* specially designed to take the Blue Riband, but was unable to pa[y] for her. In 1884 the ship was sold off to Cunard and within the yea[r] performed the feat for which she had been created. Cunard operate[d] her for a couple of years before she was rammed and sunk off Ne[w] York, without loss of life.

Joseph Bruce Ismay, Thomas Ismay's eldest son, joined th[e] Oceanic Steam Navigation Company in 1880. While Thoma[s] Ismay could fairly be described as the man who built the White Sta[r] Line into one of the greatest shipping companies ever, his son, [it] could be argued, was the man who did most to destroy it. Th[e] following year, 1881, the *Arabic* and *Coptic* became part of th[e] White Star fleet. They were intended for the Pacific routes with th[e] Occidental & Oriental Company but made a few Atlantic crossing[s] before being transferred.

Not until 1881 did Cunard manage to match the White Sta[r] liners with the introduction of the *Servia*, a steel-hulled vessel designe[d] r a speed of 17 knots, the first express transatlantic liner. The following year a sister ship, *Aurania*, joined the fleet. These were the most sumptuous liners yet built for the Cunard Line, although their accommodation still fell below the standards of White Star.

The Shaw Savill Line was predominantly occupied with the transportation of emigrants from Britain to Australia and New Zealand from the time it began in 1882. Shaw Savill had strong links with White Star, particularly during the early years, and worked with it in the Australian trade but it also sent liners across the Atlantic until the service was discontinued in 1976.

In March 1883 an experimental voyage by the Allan Line's *Hanoverian* was made from London to Halifax. The trial was successful and the following summer a regular Allan Line service was established using the *Lucerne* and the newly acquired *Norwegian* (formerly the Inman Line's *City of New York*) to Halifax and Montreal. A new fortnightly service between London,

Quebec and Montreal was begun in 1885, in place of the earlier service, using the *Canadian*, *Lucerne* and *Corean*.

In 1884 the Cunard Line gained the largest ships operating on the Atlantic: *Etruria* and *Umbria*. They were also the most powerful, as Cunard said with the *Great Eastern* in mind, 'for size does not always represent power, as stout men are aware'. To advertise its new liners Cunard produced a booklet entitled *An Aristocrat of the Atlantic*. Unmistakably providing a luxury service for its first class passengers, the Cunard Line offered no fewer than 10 meals a day. Some people, intent on getting their money's worth, consumed all 10.

The Allan Line's operations from Glasgow to South America were also improved in 1884 with the addition of the *Siberian* (3,904 tons) and the *Carthaginian* (4,444 tons) while the *Hibernian* and *Phoenician* provided a three-weekly service between Glasgow and Philadelphia. As the efficiency of the steamers available improved,

Left: An advertising poster for the Guion Line, which had once been very successful and had held the Blue Riband between 1879 and 1884 with its *Arizona* and *Alaska*. By the end of the 19th century the Guion Line had disappeared from the Atlantic Ocean.

Right: White Star's *Teutonic* (1889). It was normal practice for White Star to order its ships from the Harland & Wolff in batches of two or three almost identical vessels and its sister ship, *Majestic*[1] (1889), was very similar.

Below: The Allan Line's *Circassian* (1875), here seen in Liverpool Docks in 1890. The Allan Line provided a weekly service between Liverpool and Canada during the late 19th century with the *Circassian*, *Parisian*, *Polynesian*, *Sarmatian* and *Sardinian*.

OGDEN'S CIGARETTES.

THE "TEUTONIC."

it was found possible to operate the company's service from Liverpool to Canada with just five ships, the *Circassian*, *Polynesian*, *Parisian*, *Sardinian* and *Sarmatian*, instead of the six previously required.

The Canadian Pacific Steamship Company was started in 1884 by the Canadian Pacific Railroad. In 1889 it had three big new liners built for use on the transatlantic routes: *Empress of India*, *Empress of Japan* and *Empress of China*. By 1891 the *Empress of India* was making record-breaking runs on the route from Liverpool to Montreal.

In 1887 the Inman Line relinquished its part of the North Atlantic mail contract, so the subsidy was divided between Cunard and White Star. Because the Cunard Line ships sailed more often than those of White Star the subsidy was split, with Cunard taking 60% of the money.

In 1887 the Hull-based Wilson Line took over three of the five vessels belonging to the Monarch Line, which had gone into liquidation. The Allan Line took on the other two, *Assyrian Monarch*, which was renamed *Assyrian*, and *Grecian*

Monarch, which was renamed *Pomeranian*. At about the same time the *Austrian*, *Waldensian* and *Phoenician* were re-engined, the first two with triple expansion engines and the third with a quadruple expansion one. Until 1893 *Phoenician* was the only North Atlantic liner to be fitted with this type of engine, although they later became quite popular.

In 1888 the Allan Line acquired its first brand-new steamer powered by triple expansion engines: the 3,100-ton *Monte Video* and *Rosarian*. They were joined in 1891 by the 3,204-ton *Brazilian*. Although the new ships did occasionally operate on the South American routes their names suggested, they spent the greater part of their time on the North Atlantic.

By 1889 White Star was being seriously challenged on the North Atlantic by Cunard's *Umbria* and *Etruria* along with the Inman Line's *City of New York* and *City of Paris*. Competition between the big three lines, Cunard, Inman and White Star, was driving the evolution of the liner as all three companies strove for bigger, more comfortable and faster ships. White Star's answer was the *Teutonic* and *Majestic*. In 1891 *Teutonic* took the Blue Riband with an average speed of just over 20 knots. It was the last time that a White Star vessel would hold the record. In the future the line would go for a little less speed and a lot more luxury and size, a policy that would pay handsome dividends on the one hand and lead to the most famous maritime disaster in history on the other.

In March 1891 the Allan Line bought the fleet of six ships, and goodwill, of the State Line, which had been operating between Glasgow and New York with a stop at Larne thrown in. The State Line had recently gone into liquidation, so the Allan Line acquired it for

Above: Cunard's *Campania* (1893).

Right: The North German Lloyd liner *Prinzess Irene* (1900), originally used on oriental routes but transferred to the Southampton to New York run in 1903.

Left: Prinzess Alice
(1900), another North
German Lloyd liner that
served on oriental routes
for most of her time but
did make occasional
voyages to New York.

Below: A late 19th
century North German
Lloyd Line advertising
poster.

...e knock-down price of £72,000. Two of the former State Line
...hips were sold off immediately: the *State of Alabama* and the *State*
...f Pennsylvania. Two more were not what the Allan Line wanted,
...nd after one transatlantic round trip the *State of Indiana* was sold
...ff and after two trips the *State of Georgia* followed. The *State of*
...levada stayed with the Allan Line only until 1893, but the larger
...nd more modern *State of Nebraska* remained with the company
...ntil the following year. The *State of California* was still under
...onstruction at the time of the take-over but in due course she too
...ined the fleet. The Glasgow to New York service was continued
...nder the name 'Allan State Line'.

   Although the Canadian Government wanted the Allan Line to
...troduce an express service using bigger and faster vessels, as were
...onstantly coming into service with other lines, the management
...ad other ideas. They were perfectly happy with relatively small,
...nder 5,000-ton, ships. Unfortunately this attitude brought the
...ompany into conflict with the Canadian Government, which
...hreatened to withdraw its lucrative mail contracts. The knock-
...n effect was that the line lost a little of its confidence in the
...uture and cut back on its building programme. Nevertheless
...he 4,800-ton *Mongolian* was completed in 1891 for use on
...he Canadian run with *Circassian*, *Parisian* and *Sardinian*.
...olynesian was withdrawn from service and rebuilt as the
...,522-ton *Laurentian*. She re-entered service as primarily an
...migrant ship in 1892, having no fewer than 1,000 berths in
...eerage but only 36 in first class.

   The early 1890s saw the peak of the Allan Line's achievements.
...n 1891 the line was operating as many as 37 ships, adding up to
...20,000 gross register tons, on eight distinct routes. These were the
...veekly services between Liverpool, Quebec and Montreal;
...Glasgow, Quebec and Montreal; and Glasgow and New York. The
...ine's fortnightly services were Liverpool, St John's
...Newfoundland), Halifax and Baltimore; Glasgow and Boston;
...Glasgow, Halifax and Philadelphia; and London, Quebec and
...Montreal. On a monthly basis the Allan Line also ran a service
...etween Glasgow, Montevideo and Buenos Aires. It was too good
...o last, and the Allan Line began a long slow decline.

   Many of the Allan Line's vessels were getting a bit long in the
tooth. Almost half of them were more than 20 years old and some
were over 30. At the end of 1892 the Liverpool, St John's, Halifax
and Baltimore route was axed. From 1893 vessels on the Glasgow
to Philadelphia run began stopping off at these other points. The
old *Nova Scotia* was sold off. The service between Glasgow and
New York was maintained by the *State of California*, *State of*
Nebraska, *Corean*, *Siberian* and *Norwegian*.

Left: The *City of New York* (1888), bought from the Inman Line by the American Line in 1893. This ship was almost in collision with the *Titanic* at the start of that liner's disastrous maiden voyage on 10 April 1912. Unfortunately the collision was averted and *Titanic's* voyage was delayed by only one hour.

AMERICAN LINE

S.M.S.S. ST. PAUL AT SEA

In response to Inman's *City of Paris²* and White Star's *Teutonic*, Cunard commissioned what were to be the greatest liners the world had seen up to that time: *Campania* and *Lucania*. They were record breakers right from the start and joined the line in April and September 1893 respectively. *Campania*, illustrating how far accommodation aboard the liners had come from the early days, had electric lighting throughout, coal fires with Anglo-Persian tiles around the hearths, ottomans and revolving chairs, and an organ with gilded pipes. The two ships reigned supreme for four years until Norddeutscher Lloyd brought in its *Kaiser Wilhelm der Grosse* in 1897.

On 27 January 1893 the Allan liner *Pomeranian* set out on an Atlantic voyage. A few days later she was struck by an enormous wave which carried away her bridge, chart house and fore-deck saloon. The captain and a passenger died of the injuries they received and another 10 people were drowned. Only the magnificent seamanship of the chief officer saved the vessel from complete destruction and he managed to nurse the stricken vessel back to the Clyde. The *Pomeranian* needed a complete refit, so she was sold off.

The *Carinthia* had joined the Cunard Line in 1895, and in 1898 the *Ultonia* entered service with Cunard on its Boston service, having been purchased on the stocks.

The year of Queen Victoria's diamond jubilee, 1897, saw the arrival of the Norddeutscher Lloyd liner *Kaiser Wilhelm der Grosse* on the North Atlantic route. With her two pairs of funnels this distinctive liner was bigger and faster than anything owned by either White Star or Cunard. The appearance of the new German vessel at such a time wounded British pride. White Star's answer was the

Oceanic², the first ship to exceed Brunel's *Great Eastern* in length (though not in tonnage).

In 1897 the Allan Line bought the three 4,000-ton twin-screw steamers *Tower Hill*, *Ludgate Hill* and *Richmond Hill* from W. B. Hill and W. H. Nott and renamed them *Turanian*, *Livonia* and *Roumanian*. The new additions to the Allan Line fleet were put into service on the Glasgow to New York run. The *State of California* was moved to the Liverpool to Canada run and in 1898 she was renamed *Californian*.

During the 1880s and 90s the average size of new liners entering service on the North Atlantic had grown enormously, as had their cost. As a result, the Allan Line completely reorganised itself in 1897. The original name 'Montreal Ocean Steamship Company' was dropped and a new company, the 'Allan Line Steamship Company Limited' was formed with £600,000 capital. Shortly afterwards an order for three new large liners was placed.

The first of the new Allan Line ships was the 7,441-ton, single-screw *Castilian*, which turned out to be anything but a lucky ship.

...fax on her maiden voyage on
...l in the Bay of Fundy during the
...bad matters worse, the line's old
...han 150 round trips across the
...n service for a major refit a couple
...ously life in the old *Parisian* yet
...t a new record for the route from
...Race of 8 days 21 hours and
...Tory Island to Cape Race was a
...fill in for the *Castilian* the 5,086-
...aw Savill & Albion for six round
...herly a Cunard vessel, was bought
...Line. With no better luck than the
...near Sorel Point, Quebec, on her
...ly damaged that, when she was
...bourg and scrapped.
...olved in a rather unusual project in
...ered to transport 537 reindeer, 418
...reindeer sleds, 511 sets of

harness and 3,500 bags of moss to feed the animals to the USA. Along with the animals and other equipment were herders, drivers and their families: 113 people in all. From this single voyage came the American Government's reindeer herd.

The *Ormiston* was bought in from R. and C. Allan in 1899 and her name was changed to *Orcadian*. The next vessel to join the line was the large twin screwed *Bavarian*, capable of a service speed of 16 knots and of carrying 1,000 steerage, 200 second and 240 first class passengers. Hardly had the ship entered service than she was requisitioned by the British Government to transport troops to South Africa to fight the Boers. She was not returned until the war was over and made her first postwar voyage for the Allan Line in October 1902. To help fill the gap the line brought a sister ship, the 10,576-ton *Tunisian*, into service in April 1900.

White Star's *Oceanic*[2] was launched in 1899, the same year that Thomas Ismay died. She was the last ship he had ordered from Harland & Wolff, although there was to have been a sister ship, *Olympic*, but this was cancelled. The management of the line passed to Joseph Bruce Ismay. Before his death Thomas Ismay had ordered the plans for an even larger vessel, *Celtic*, to be drawn up. J. Bruce Ismay (as he was styled) went ahead with the new liner and *Celtic* was launched in 1901. She was the largest ship in the world and the first to exceed 20,000 gross register tons.

1900 saw two specially designed vessels join the Cunard fleet: *Ivernia* and *Saxonia*. These ships were not designed to be particularly fast but to be capable of carrying 2,300 passengers and 14,000 tons of cargo apiece.

In 1900 the Allan Line purchased the 4,309-ton *Ontarian* while she was still on the stocks. Next came three new 6,000-ton plus steamers: the *Sicilian*, *Corinthian*[2] and slightly larger, at almost 7,000-tons, *Pretorian*. Continued on page 30.

AMERICAN LINE.

U.S.M.S.S. ST PAUL LEAVING NEW YORK FOR SOUTHAMPTON.

Left and above: The American Line's *St Paul* (1895) was the first Atlantic liner to be permanently fitted with Marconi wireless equipment in 1898. On 25 April 1908 the *St Paul*, under the control of pilot George Bowyer, rammed the Royal Navy's cruiser *Gladiator* in a snowstorm, just off Yarmouth. The cruiser had to be beached to prevent her from sinking; 27 naval personnel were killed.

Right: St Louis (1895), the American Line sister ship to the *St Paul*.

S.S. St. Louis

This spread:
Colourful advertising
cards issued at the
beginning of the
20th century by
the Belgian
Red Star Line.

ss Afric

Oakley Photo Copyright   Troops Embarking.   Netley. Southampton.

ALLAN LINE Royal Mail S.S.

on Board
S.S. Tunisian

April 3rd

Dear Annie. We have arrived off the coast of Ireland it is very mountainous, we have had a very nice voyage so far, only the sea is too calm. No one has been bad yet. Cyril

Top: White Star's *Afric* (1898) embarking troops at Southampton.

Above: The Allan Line's *Tunisian* (1900).

This page: Tunisian in the River Mersey. In 1922, in Canadian Pacific Line service, the *Tunisian* was renamed *Marburn*.

R.M.S. "Tunisian"

Hands across the Sea

S.S. TUNISIAN

"HANDS ACROSS THE SEA."

S.S. SAXONIA. (CUNARD LINE.) 14,280 TONS

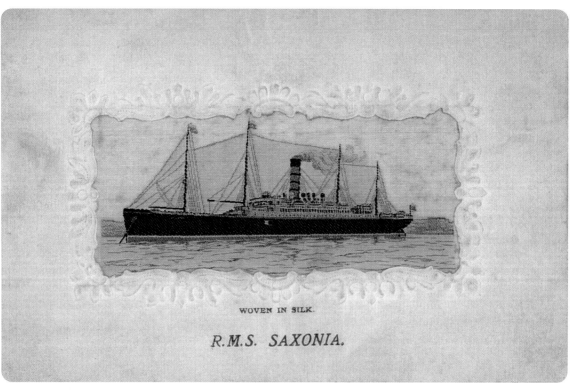

WOVEN IN SILK.

R.M.S. SAXONIA.

Top: The Elder Dempster Line vessel *Lake Champlain*
(1900), the first British liner fitted with Marconi wireless
equipment.

Above: White Star's *Arabic*[2] (1902) in the River Mersey
with the tender *Magnetic* alongside. *Arabic* was torpedoed
and sunk by a German U-boat in 1915, just three weeks
before and in the same place as *Lusitania*.

Right: John Pierpont Morgan, the American financier who
tried to buy up all of the major shipping lines on the North
Atlantic in the early 1900s when he set up his cartel,
International Mercantile Marine.

Above: North German Lloyd's *Kaiser Wilhelm II* (1902), which operated between Bremen and New York, calling at Southampton and Plymouth.

Right: Cunard liner *Caronia[1]* (1905) at Liverpool's Prince's Landing Stage. *Caronia* served with distinction as an armed merchant cruiser during World War 1.

Because of the need to transport troops to South Africa to fig the Boer War, the British Government took over the new *Sicilia* and *Bavarian* along with the *Mongolian*, *Siberian*, *Carthaginia Sardinian*, *Laurentian* and *Pomeranian* as transports. Most of the vessels were required to make only one journey as troopships. S Cunard mail steamers were taken over by the British government f service during the Boer War. During her war service *Carinthia* wa wrecked while transporting mules from New Orleans to Cape Tow

The Allan Line *Californian* had run aground off Portland i February 1900 and looked like becoming a total loss. However, sh was eventually refloated and after extensive repairs made fo Atlantic crossings before being sold off to the New York & Puer Rican Line.

In 1901 the Allan and Furness Lines arranged to share a ma service to St John's, Newfoundland, with Furness contributing th *Ulunda* and *Damara*. For this one venture the Furness Allan Lin came into being. Also in 1901, pending the arrival of a new shij the Allan Line chartered the 7,801-ton *Ruapehu* from the Ne Zealand Shipping Company, renaming the vessel *Australasian* eve though she made only five complete voyages between Liverpoo Montreal and Quebec for the line. Her replacement, the brand-ne twin-screw, four-masted, 8,268-ton *Ionian* came into service on th Liverpool to Canada route. She was an immediate success an became one of the best earners the line owned.

In 1893, while on an Atlantic crossing, a fellow passenger ha asked the American financier John Pierpont Morgan if he thought possible for one organisation to buy up all of the passenger line operating on the North Atlantic so that they could all make a prof rather than competing with one another. 'Ought to be,' wa organ's response, but almost 10 years were to elapse before he got ound to doing anything with the idea. Then, just after the Boer ar, J. P. Morgan began to put together an enormous North Atlantic ipping cartel, the International Mercantile Marine Company, or MM for short. His intention was to buy up all of the shipping lines erating between Europe and the United States but due to vernment intervention by Britain and Germany he failed to acquire unard, Hamburg Amerika and North German Lloyd. In 1902, wever, White Star was taken over by IMM. Although the take-er was initially resisted by Ismay, he changed his mind when organ offered to pay £10 million for the line. At the annual general eeting in May 1902, 75% of the shareholders, including J. Bruce may, voted to accept Morgan's offer. Morgan also managed to gain ntrol of the Dominion, Atlantic Transport, Leyland, British and orth Atlantic, American, and Red Star Lines so that IMM ntrolled more Atlantic shipping than any other line. In 1902 organ's ships carried 64,738 passengers. The Hamburg Amerika d North German Lloyd lines carried 66,838 passengers, while nchor, Cunard and the French Line carried 59,506.

Although IMM was mainly interested in the North Atlantic ade, the Leyland Line had strong ties with the Mediterranean. hese were formed into another distinct company, the Ellerman ne. White Star had always had an interest in the Antipodean ade and had long been in collaboration with the Shaw Savill & lbion Line in that respect. Under IMM this collaboration became en closer and *Athenic*, *Corinthic* and *Ionic* were handed over.

Eventually Shaw Savill even began to use the famous White Star 'ic' in its own ship's names.

Following the creation of IMM the British Government came to an agreement with Cunard that in return for the line remaining British it would be granted a loan of more than £2.5 million to build two new record-breaking ships. In addition, the government would also pay the line a subsidy of £150,000 a year for 20 years to cover its additional costs in running the two new super-liners, which had to be built to Admiralty specifications for service as armed merchant cruisers in the event of war. The two vessels were to be the *Lusitania* and *Mauretania*. Another new Cunard ship was the vessel which was to save 705 people from the *Titanic*, the *Carpathia*, which also entered service with Cunard in 1902.

In 1902 the 6,859-ton *Huronian*, which had been purchased only the year before from the Anchor Line, became the only Allan Line steamer ever to disappear without trace, even though the Royal Navy sent out the cruisers *Bellona* and *Thames* to search the North Atlantic for her.

In 1903 the *Aurania* joined Cunard though not for service on the regular North Atlantic run but on the route from Fiume to New York via Trieste and Venice. Two years later two new sister ships entered service: *Caronia* and *Carmania*. *Carmania* was equipped with Parsons turbine engines, while *Caronia* had quadruple expansion engines. *Carmania* turned out to be about 1½ knots faster than her sister for the same expenditure in coal, so from then onwards all of Cunard's new large vessels would be turbine-driven.

S. S. Caronia, Liverpool.

1028 *La Savoie*. L.V. & Cⁱᵉ

Top left: The French liner *La Savoie* (1901) which operated between Le Havre and New York.

Left: The French liner *La Touraine*.

Top right: The White Star liner *Baltic*² (1904) in the Mersey, being led by *Magnetic*.

Above right: The German liner *Kronprinzessin Cecilie* entering dock at Southampton.

GOOD AND BAD TIMES

edric, sister ship to *Celtic* and the second of a class that was to become known as the 'Big Four', joined White Star's North Atlantic service in 1903. In the same year the old *Britannic²* was sold for scrap. To replace *Britannic* on the Liverpool to New York route the Atlantic Transport Line's *Minnewaska* was transferred to White Star and renamed *Arabic²*. The Dominion Line contributed the *Commonwealth* as *Canopic*, *New England* as *Romanic*, *Columbus* as *Republic²* and *Mayflower* as *Cretic*. The Leyland Line was also obliged to hand over four of its best ships to White Star: *American* as *Cufic²* and *European* as *Tropic²*; Leyland's cargo vessels *Victorian* and *Armenian* were handed over without a change of name.

So successful was the Canadian Pacific Line that in 1903 it bought the Elder Dempster Beaver Line's entire fleet of 15 ships. With the additional vessels Canadian Pacific was able to set up a regular transatlantic service operating out of Liverpool, London and Avonmouth (Bristol), sailing to Canada. In 1904 the company decided to include another port of call, Antwerp, for its four liners operating out of London. As is so often the case with the shipping business, just when everything seemed to be going so well, disaster struck. The *Monterey* was lost in the St Lawrence estuary in July 1903.

In the period between 1896 and 1902 a dozen Allan Line steamers went to the scrapyard. This left just 23 passenger vessels and four cargo ships in the line's service. This wholesale disposal ships left the line with too few vessels to meet its commitments a two vessels had to be chartered to maintain services; these were t City Line's 4,548-ton *City of Bombay* and the *City of Vienna*. T following year things took a turn for the worse, if that was possib with Canadian Pacific's acquisition of Elder Dempster. The Alla Line fought back in 1904 by winning a new contract for ma between Britain and Canada, and another in 1905 to carry ma from France to Canada. These contracts enabled the line advertise itself as the only company with government contracts f Canadian mails.

White Star's *Baltic²* was commissioned in 1904. Because 20 had been added to her length while she was being built she was t largest ship in the world. In 1905 the *Germanic* was transferred the Dominion Line and renamed *Ottawa*. IMM had not been t commercial success that J. P. Morgan had hoped for and as t chairman, Clement Griscom, was in poor health, the financier aske J. Bruce Ismay to take over. At first Ismay was not too keen but t promise of complete control over IMM and a salary of £20,000 year changed his mind. The number of people wanting to cross t Atlantic had begun to fall off and in the early autumn of 190 White Star abandoned its service to San Francisco. The *Doric* too the final sailing from that port.

Left: The drawing office at Harland & Wolff's Belfast shipyard where so many transatlantic liners were designed.

Right: Driving in wedges to transfer a ship's weight from the keel blocks to the launching cradle shortly before a ship wa slipped into the water in the early 1900s

S. S. EMPRESS OF IRELAND.

Left: Caronia[1] under way in the Mersey.

Below left: Canadian Pacific's *Empress of Ireland* (1906), which sailed on the Quebec–Liverpool route.

Right: A diagram showing the development in the size of steamships during the period 1819–1907.

In 1903 the Allan line had ordered two new turbine-driven vessels: the 10,635-ton *Victorian* and the 10,757-ton *Virginian*. The *Victorian*, which entered service on 23 March 1905, was the first turbine-driven steamer on the North Atlantic and one of the fastest vessels in the world. *Virginian* entered service on 6 April 1905. In May of the following year she set a new record by steaming from Liverpool to Rimouski, in the St Lawrence, in 5 days, 20 hours and 10 minutes. She took the eastbound record two months later with a time of 6 days, 5 hours for the same route. The speed of the new ships meant that they could maintain a service on their own and that other, older, vessels were no longer required. Consequently the *Peruvian*, *Phoenician* and *Austrian* were scrapped. The Allan Line's *Bavarian* ran aground in the St Lawrence River near Quebec on 3 November 1905. The ship was a complete loss and was broken up where she was, without ever being refloated.

By 1900 the Cunard Line owned only eight ships and the situation remained much the same until 1907 when the *Lusitania* and *Mauretania* came into service, quickly followed by *Aquitania*. These ships were by far the biggest and fastest liners in the world at that time. *Lusitania* was commissioned on 28 July 1907 and on her second transatlantic voyage took the Blue Riband with an average speed of 25 knots. Four months later *Mauretania*, the second of the sisters, took the record at 26 knots. She would hold the Blue Riband for an astonishing 22 years.

The arrival of these two super-liners sparked off the need to respond in the Hamburg Amerika and White Star Lines. Hamburg Amerika commissioned the 40,000-ton-plus *Bismarck* and *Imperator*. White Star's answer was to build three new ships of its own, each to be far more opulent and half again as big as the new Cunard liners. Thus the 'Olympic' class, of which *Titanic* was the second, was conceived.

Adriatic[2], the last of the 'Big Four' joined the White Star fleet in 1907 and a whole new service was introduced for these prestigious vessels from Southampton to New York, calling at Cherbourg and Queenstown (now Cobh) in Ireland. No sooner had the new service begun than White Star announced its intention to replace the new ships with the even larger 'Olympics'. This new class would consist of the *Olympic*, *Titanic* and *Gigantic* (the name of the proposed *Gigantic* was changed before the vessel was built to *Britannic*[2]). The cost of these new ships was enormous at £1.5 million apiece.

On 22 January 1909 the *Republic* left New York for Genoa carrying relief supplies for the victims of a recent earthquake in Italy. During the night the ship ran into thick fog but Captain William Inman Sealby pressed on regardless. Unknown to Captain Sealby

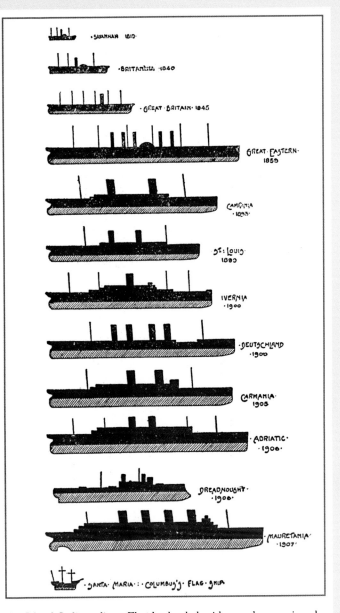

the Lloyd Italiano liner *Florida*, loaded with people escaping the hardships brought about by the Italian earthquake, was approaching through the fog. Captain Ruspini of the *Florida* was also maintaining his speed. Both vessels were sounding their fog-horns at regular intervals but to no useful purpose.

At about 5.45am on 23 January the *Florida* ran into the *Republic's* port side just aft of the funnel before disappearing again into the fog. The impact tore a hole in the White Star ship's side that reached from her promenade deck to well below the waterline. About 30ft of *Florida's* bow had crumpled up like the bellows of a concertina and her forward two compartments had flooded. *Republic's* wireless cabin had been destroyed in the collision but her operator, Jack Binns, discovered that the wireless itself was still operable, after a fashion. Although the ship's electrical power failed as the engine room flooded and short-circuited the dynamos, there were emergency batteries if Binns could find them in the dark. The batteries were discovered in a flooded adjacent compartment and Binns had to dive for them. Nevertheless, within half an hour of the collision Jack Binns was transmitting a distress call.

Republic was clearly sinking and Captain Sealby knew that there were nothing like enough lifeboats to accommodate the people he had aboard. Then Florida reappeared and it was decided to transfer Republic's people to her as, although badly damaged, she was in no immediate danger of sinking. Meanwhile Binns had managed to contact another White Star liner, Baltic,

and she was hurrying to the rescue. Eventually, after a hazardou time spent searching for the stricken Republic in the dense fog, about 3.00pm, Baltic arrived. All of the passengers and crew th could be spared were transferred from both Republic and Florid to Baltic. Binns' persistence with the wireless had paid dividend and looked as if it might pay more. He had managed t communicate with the White Star Line's New York office and was sending a couple of salvage tugs in the hope that the Republi could be towed into shallow water and beached before sh foundered. At long last the revenue cutte Gresham arrived and the tow began, but was useless. The waterlogged liner wa too heavy to be towed at any appreciabl speed and it had covered less than 1 miles when, at shortly before 9.00pm o 24 January, Republic finally sank. Sh was replaced on the route by th Zeelandic.

Two ships originally laid down fo the Dominion Line as Alberta an Albany were taken over by White Sta while still on the stocks as th Laurentic and Megantic, beginning collaboration known as the Whit Star Dominion Line Joint Servic which continued until 1926.

Continued on page 47.

Above: The Allan liner *Virginian* (1905).

Right: The Allan liner *Victorian* (1905) in the River Mersey.

Above: Another Allan Line steamer, the *Corsican* (1907).

Below: The Cunard liner *Caronia* (1905).

Cunard Liner "LUSITANIA" (Turbine).

32,000 Tons ; 68,000 H.P. ; Speed 26¼ knots
Length 787 ft. ; Breadth 88 ft. ; Depth 60 ft.

CUNARD LINE.

LUSITANIA

S.S. LUSITANIA Turbine

Top and above: The Cunard liner *Lusitania* (1907), the first of a new
class of express super-liner for the North Atlantic service.

below and bottom: The second of the new Cunard express liners, and one of the most successful ships of all time, *Mauretania* (1907).

R.M.S. "Mauretania."

33,200 Tons. 68,000 h.p.
790 ft. Long; 88 ft. Broad.
60½ ft. Deep.

Copyright H.L & Co.L.

Cunard Line R.M.S.
"Mauretania".

Left: A 1908 Cunard Line publicity card advertising the new express super-liners.

Below: A colour view of the first class lounge aboard *Mauretania.*

Bottom: Lusitania (1907) at Queenstown (Cobh) on her way to New York in about 1912.

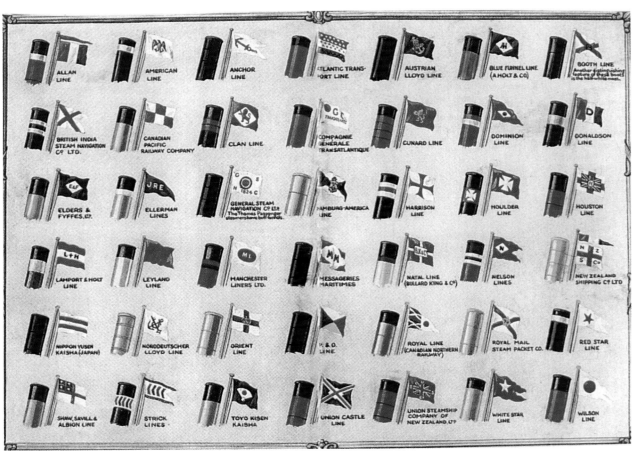

Within the image, the following shipping line labels appear:

ALLAN LINE	AMERICAN LINE	ANCHOR LINE	ATLANTIC TRANSPORT LINE	AUSTRIAN LLOYD LINE	BLUE FUNNEL LINE (A. HOLT & CO)	BOOTH LINE
BRITISH INDIA STEAM NAVIGATION Cº LTD.	CANADIAN PACIFIC RAILWAY COMPANY	CLAN LINE	COMPAGNIE GÉNÉRALE TRANSATLANTIQUE	CUNARD LINE	DOMINION LINE	DONALDSON LINE
ELDERS & FYFFES, LTD.	ELLERMAN LINES	GENERAL STEAM NAVIGATION Cº LTD	HAMBURG-AMERICA LINE	HARRISON LINE	HOULDER LINE	HOUSTON LINE
LAMPORT & HOLT LINE	LEYLAND LINE	MANCHESTER LINERS LTD.	MESSAGERIES MARITIMES	NATAL LINE (BULLARD KING & Cº)	NELSON LINES	NEW ZEALAND SHIPPING Cº LTD
NIPPON YUSEN KAISHA (JAPAN)	NORDDEUTSCHER LLOYD LINE	ORIENT LINE	P. & O. LINE	ROYAL LINE (CANADIAN NORTHERN RAILWAY)	ROYAL MAIL STEAM PACKET CO.	RED STAR LINE
SHAW, SAVILL & ALBION LINE	STRICK LINES	TOYO KISEN KAISHA	UNION CASTLE LINE	UNION STEAMSHIP COMPANY OF NEW ZEALAND, LTD	WHITE STAR LINE	WILSON LINE

Above: The house flags and funnel markings of the major shipping lines in the period leading up to the Great War.

Left: White Star's *Adriatic*[2] (1907) served on the Liverpool to New York route.

Left: A Cunard menu cover from *Lusitania* some time about 1910.

Right: Front page of the *Daily Mirror*, 29 July 1910. Dr Hawley Harvey Crippen, who had murdered his wife before fleeing England aboard the steamer *Montrose* with his lady friend, Ethel Le Neve, is identified and a wireless signal sent to Britain to that effect. Acting on that wireless signal Inspector Walter Dew of Scotland Yard booked passage on the much faster White Star liner *Laurentic* and intercepted Crippen on his arrival in Canada. Crippen was duly hanged.

The Daily Mirror

THE MORNING JOURNAL WITH THE SECOND LARGEST NET SALE

No. 2,108.

Registered at the G.P.O.
as a Newspaper.

FRIDAY, JULY 29, 1910

One Halfpenny.

"CRIPPEN BEYOND A DOUBT"—YESTERDAY'S WIRELESS MESSAGE FROM CAPTAIN KENDALL, OF THE STEAMER MONTROSE.

Mr. Llewellyn Jones, Marconi operator on the Montrose.

Inspector Dew, who will bring back the fugitives.

Captain Kendall, of the steamer Montrose.

The steamer Montrose, on board which are Crippen and Miss Le Neve.

Miss Le Neve, who accompanies "Dr." Crippen dressed as a boy.

Chart showing the positions of the Montrose and the Laurentic.

"Dr." Crippen, who is now definitely said to be on the Montrose.

A wireless message was received yesterday from Captain Kendall, of the steamer Montrose, which stated that the identity of the suspected passengers on the ship had been established "beyond a doubt." It will be remembered that two passengers who entered their names on embarking on the Montrose at Antwerp as "Mr. Robinson and son" were suspected as being "Dr." Crippen and Miss Le Neve, for whom a world-wide search was being made, and as a result of a wireless message from the captain Inspector Dew, of Scotland Yard, was sent to overtake the suspects on the faster steamer Laurentic.

White Star Liner
R.M.S. "Laurentic."
Triple Screw.

15340 Tons.   565 Feet Long.
67½ Feet Deep.

Left: The White Star liner *Laurentic*[1] (1908). In 1917, while carrying £5 million worth of gold, *Laurentic* struck two mines and sank off Northern Ireland; 354 people were lost. After the war, in a remarkable salvage operation, 95% of the gold was recovered.

Above right: White Star's *Megantic* (1908), sister ship to *Laurentic*[1]. Both vessels were used primarily on the Liverpool to Canada route.

Right: Megantic[1] departs Liverpool.

Between 1908 and 1912 the Allan Line scrapped a number of older vessels. The *Brazilian* was sold off, and the *Laurentian* was wrecked in Trepassey Bay, Newfoundland, on 6 September 1909. The *Laurentian* was the 20th ship that the line had lost. During 1910 the Allan Line began to collaborate with the Canadian Pacific Line, and it was soon apparent that the lines were to merge. In reality Canadian Pacific had gained complete control of the Allan Line the previous year and vessels belonging to both companies began to operate on one another's routes. In 1911 the Allan Line bought in the 10,322-ton Holland America liner *Statendam* and renamed her *Scotian*. The following year the 12,099-ton *Romanic* was purchased from the White Star line and renamed *Scandinavian[2]*. She, like many other Allan Line steamers, would carry only second and third class passengers.

In 1911 and 1912 the *Franconia* and *Laconia* came into service with Cunard on its Liverpool to Boston route. These two vessels, demonstrating that the management at Cunard had its fingers on the pulse of the transatlantic passenger trade, were also designed to serve as cruise liners during the winter months. In 1911 Cunard bought out the Canadian Thompson Line of three ships. In 1912 the company expanded again by purchasing the Glasgow-based Anchor Line.

The first of the gigantic new 'Olympic' class ships came into White Star service in early June 1911. The *Olympic* at 45,324 gross register tons and almost 900ft in length was the largest vessel in the world, although at a modest 22 knots by no means the fastest. She was the first of three sisters, each a little bigger than the last. At the end of her first Atlantic voyage the *Olympic* collided with and badly damaged the New York harbour tug *O. L. Hallenbeck*. At the beginning of her fifth round trip, on 20 September 1911, as she was leaving Southampton Water *Olympic* was rammed in the starboard quarter by the Royal Navy's armoured cruiser HMS *Hawke* and severely damaged. After two months of repairs *Olympic* re-entered service. With the cost of

White Star Liner "Olympic."

Launched 20th October, 1910.
45,000 Tons ; Speed, 21-knots.
Length, 883 ft. ;
Breadth, 93 ft. ; Depth, 97 ft.

Left: White Star's answer to the Cunard super-liners was to build three of its own, the first being *Olympic* (1911).

Below left: The second White Star giant, *Titanic* (1912).

Right: The third of the *Olympic* class ships, *Britannic*[2] (1914) was immediately requisitioned by the British Government for use as a hospital ship. She struck a mine in the Aegean sea in 1916 and sank. Unlike the *Britannic* in this picture, the real ship never sailed in White Star colours.

Below right: Olympic at New York, probably at the end of her first Atlantic crossing.

WHITE STAR LINE.

building and repairing, and lost revenue while she was out of commission, the huge liner had cost the White Star Line something approaching £2 million, so the owners were understandably keen that she should start to earn her keep as soon as possible. However, the liner was damaged again, by exceptionally heavy seas, on 14 January 1912 and yet again on 24 February when she ran into what is believed to have been a submerged wreck. This latest accident damaged *Olympic's* port main propeller and necessitated another return to the builders so that a blade could be replaced. This job, which should have been completed in a single day, took a full week and caused the cancellation of another scheduled voyage.

This bad start was not the only reason why 1912 was not th White Star Line's best year. The second of the 'Olympic' cla ships, *Titanic*, set off on her maiden voyage on 10 April with mo than 2,200 passengers and crew aboard. Late in the evening 14 April she ran into an iceberg and foundered two hours an 40 minutes later, at 2.20am on 15 April 1912. The liner ha lifeboat provision for about half of those aboard but because of clas sex and racial discrimination, along with crew inefficiency an panic, many of the boats left only half full. More than 1,500 peop were lost with the *Titanic* in what must be the most famous maritim calamity in history.

R.M.S. Britannic
Length, 900 ft.
Breadth, 94 ft.
Tonnage, 50,000

R.M.S.P. & P.S.N.C.

TO SOUTH AMERICA

via France, Spain, Portugal, & Atlantic Islands

Weekly from Southampton, Liverpool & Glasgow

Tours round South America from £100 for about 10 weeks

Fortnightly from Southampton & Cherbourg to The Azores, WEST INDIES—Pacific—NEW YORK

From London to Gibraltar,

MOROCCO,

Canary Islands, &

MADEIRA.

23 days from £22

Cruises-de-Luxe by Ocean Yachting Steamer "ARCADIAN" to

NORWAY, THE BALTIC, MEDITERRANEAN, HOLY LAND, EGYPT, ETC.

From £1 a day

The Royal Mail Steam Packet Company
The Pacific Steam Navigation Company

LONDON: 18 Moorgate St., E.C., or 32 Cockspur St., S.W.
LIVERPOOL: 31 James Street.

"WARSPITE" TRAINING SHIP

MARINE SOCIETY (Instituted 1756)

President: The EARL OF ROMNEY

In 1786 the Society instituted the first training ship in this or any other Country.

On board the *Warspite* 240 poor boys of good character only are annually trained, exclusively for the Sea Services. This number could be increased to 400 if additional funds were forthcoming.

From 1756 to 1911 over 66,200 boys have been sent to sea, and of these 37,500 joined the Mercantile Marine.

The *Society* appeals most earnestly for Funds to all interested in the manning of the Sea Services.

The smallest contributions will be thankfully received, and should be sent to—

The SECRETARY, MARINE SOCIETY,
CLARK'S PLACE, BISHOPSGATE, E.C.

Far left: Royal Mail Steam Packet Company advertisement from 1911.

Left: A 1911 training card. Many professional seamen began their careers by learning the rudiments of their trade aboard training ships like *Warspite*.

Below left: Advertising card for the training ship *Indefatigable*, moored in the River Mersey.

Below: Another advertising card, this time for the officer training ship *Conway* which was moored at Liverpool.

LIVERPOOL TRAINING SHIP "INDEFATIGABLE"

Over 4,000 boys trained and sent to sea

Patron: HIS MAJESTY THE KING.
Chairman: ARTHUR W. BIBBY, Esq.
Hon. Treasurer: T. ROYDEN, Esq., J.P.

THIS Institution was established in 1865 to train lads for the Merchant Service, and only Good Lads of the Non-criminal Class, who desire to adopt the sea as a profession, are eligible for admission, preference being given to the claims of orphans or sons of seafaring men connected with the port of Liverpool.

The age at which boys are received is from 13 to 15 years, and applicants must come up to the following standard of height:—Between 13 and 13½ years of age, 4 ft. 7 in.; 13½ and 14, 4 ft. 8 in.; 14 and 14½, 4 ft. 10 in.; 14½ and 15, 5 ft. Each candidate must submit to a medical examination; have good eyesight, and will only be received if found physically fitted for a seafaring life.

Boys with Fathers living, or those not belonging to Liverpool, are admitted upon relatives or friends paying cost of maintenance and providing Outfit on going to sea.

Application for admission to be made to the Secretary,
Mr. W. THWAITES, 11 Lord Street, Liverpool.

H.M.S. "CONWAY" SCHOOLSHIP

MOORED IN THE MERSEY

Designed primarily to give a sound GENERAL and TECHNICAL EDUCATION to boys desirous of becoming Officers in the Mercantile Marine Service. Six nominations Annually (two each term) to the R.N. College, Dartmouth. Two years on the "Conway" count for apprenticeship as one year's sea service. Carpenters' and Engine Fitter's Shops, etc. Extensive Playing Fields on shore.

Fees £22 15s. per term

For Prospectus apply to
Commander H. W. BROADBENT, R.D., R.N.R.,
H.M.S. "Conway," Rock Ferry, Cheshire.

H.M. Training Ships on Mersey, Liverpool.

H.M.S. CONWAY, MENAI BRIDGE   23605

Above: Three training ships moored in the River Mersey at Liverpool. On the left is the *St Vincent*, which catered for seamen's orphans. In the centre is the *Conway*, for officer cadets. On the right is *Indefatigable*, which looked after the sons of Liverpool sailors.

Left: The end of the *Conway*. She was beached in North Wales, not far from the Menai Bridge, and broken up in the 1950s.

As a result of the *Titanic* disaster, regulations were changed so that in future there would by lifeboat provision for all aboard, which sounds like a good idea but actually is still inadequate. More often than not, as a ship sinks it lists to one side or the other, which makes it impossible to lower the boats on the higher side of the vessel. The 'Olympic' class ships were specially designed so that should they be severely damaged, they would not heel over and all the boats could be lowered. The modern regulations, which do not call for ships that will remain upright as they sink, mean that the lifeboat situation remains practically unchanged. On the positive side, wireless sets are now manned for 24 hours a day and there is a North Atlantic Ice Patrol that reports on the quantities and positions of icebergs in that ocean. The iceberg that the *Titanic* struck was in the general position where bergs had been reported to her on several occasions on 14 April and in the more precise position reported some two hours before the collision. Clearly, knowing the position of an iceberg is no guarantee that a ship will not run into it.

At the end of 1912 the *Olympic* was again returned to the builders, this time for alterations that would ensure that the damage that had presumably sunk her sister could not sink her. The third sister ship, *Britannic*[2], was altered so that she too could survive damage similar to that sustained by *Titanic*.

Royal Liver Buildings and Dock Offices, Liverpool

R.M.S. "Lusitania" at Landing Stage, Liverpool

Landing Stage from South, Liverpool

TRACK CHART R.M.S.P.

THE ROYAL MAIL STEAM PACKET Cᵒ

Fast Mail Services between

EUROPE, WEST INDIES & NEW YORK, PACIFIC, CENTRAL AMERICA &C.

ARGENTINA & BRAZIL. SPAIN & PORTUGAL.

CUBA & MEXICO. MEDITERRANEAN, EGYPT & AUSTRALIA

Above: An unusual postcard from about 1912 showing Liverpool pierhead in 1908, *Lusitania* berthed at Liverpool in about 1912 and an Allan liner in the River Mersey.

Above right: Cover of a Royal Mail Steam Packet Company North Atlantic Track Chart from about 1913 and RMSP North Atlantic chart showing the routes followed, east- and westbound.

Right: The French liner *France* (1912) served on the Le Havre to New York route.

C. V. 10 - LE HAVRE — Le Transatlantique "France" Longueur, 218 m., largeur, 23 m. jaugeant 27.000 tonnes 4 hélices actionnées par des turbines vitesse, 23 nœuds, passagers, 2.000

"A PROVENCE"

Left: Another French liner, *La Provence* (1912), which was one of the ships that picked up *Titanic's* distress calls on the night of 14–15 April 1912.

Below: First class dinner menu from the Royal Mail Steam Packet Company's *Desna* for 15 September 1913.

The fortunes of the Allan Line were in decline by 1913 when the South American service, along with the goodwill attaching to it, was sold to the Donaldson Line. As well as the service, Donaldson also took over the *Orcadian* and *Ontarian*. On 29 May 1914 the Canadian Pacific line had its own version of the *Titanic* disaster. The *Empress of Ireland* was rammed in the St Lawrence Seaway and sank with the loss of 1,053 passengers and crew. Her place in the company's fleet was taken by the Allan Line's *Virginian*. In 1914 the Allan Line took delivery of two new vessels: the 18,481-ton *Alsatian* and the 17,515-ton *Calgarian*. These vessels are notable as being the first four-screw turbine-driven ships with cruiser sterns (without the overhanging sterns of other vessels of the time) to operate on the North Atlantic. In the same year the old *Parisian* was scrapped.

On 31 May 1914 the *Aquitania* began her maiden voyage across the Atlantic. Without doubt one of the best looking of the more than 200 ships that have sailed under the Cunard flag, *Aquitania* was also one of the longest lived, remaining with the line until 1950.

White Star had replaced *Titanic* on the North Atlantic route between Southampton and New York with the ageing *Majestic*, but only as a temporary measure. In 1914 she was replaced by the *Vaderland* and *Zeeland*, brought in from the Red Star Line. In August, however, World War 1 began and shortly afterwards the vessel's names, which sounded too Germanic, were changed to *Southland* and *Northland*. *Cedric*, *Celtic*[2], *Teutonic* and *Oceanic*[2] were taken over by the Royal Navy for use as armed merchant cruisers. On 8 September, shortly after entering service as a warship, *Oceanic* ran aground in broad daylight on the Shaalds of Foula off the Shetland Isles and was wrecked. To replace the ships requisitioned for war service the *Lapland* was brought in from the Red Star Line.

R.M.S.P "DESNA."
September 15th, 1913

MENU.

Dinner

Hors d'Œuvres

Consomme D'Esclignac

Potage Parmentier

Salmon, Ravigotê Sauce

Tomatoes, Provencale
Braised Sweetbreads, St. Cloud

Sirloin of Beef, Hominy Croquettes
Roast Turkey, Chipolata

Vegetable Marrow
Browned and Boiled Potatoes

Cabinet Pudding
Snow Cakes

Cheese   Coffee
          Dessert

Above: White Star's *Titanic* (1912) is seen off Cowes.

Above right: White Star's *Magazine cover*

Right: White Star's *Olympic* First class smoking room.

Below right: Some postcards which purported to show *Titanic* in fact showed her sister ship *Olympic*, as in this example.

R.M.S. TITANIC.

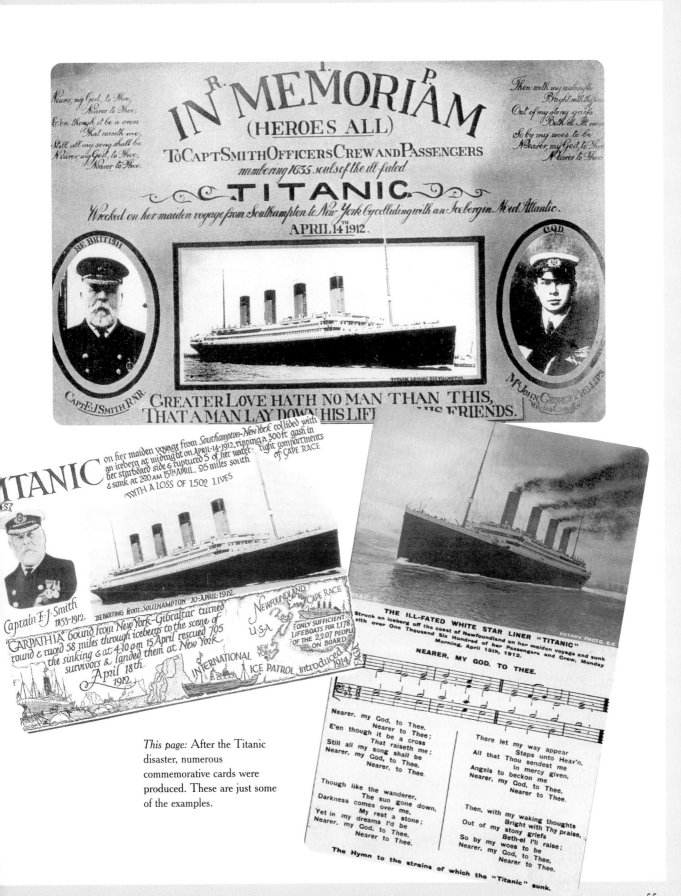

This page: After the Titanic disaster, numerous commemorative cards were produced. These are just some of the examples.

Right: Three *Titanic* commemorative cards.

Below: A postcard of Gladstone Dock at Liverpool, with the Cunard liner *Aquitania* berthed in the foreground. Built to fulfil the demands of the shipping companies for larger accommodation for their transatlantic liners, Gladstone Dock was first opened in 1913 although the new dock complex was not completed until the 1920s.

Below right: The Allan liner *Virginian* received the last wireless transmissions from the *Titanic*.

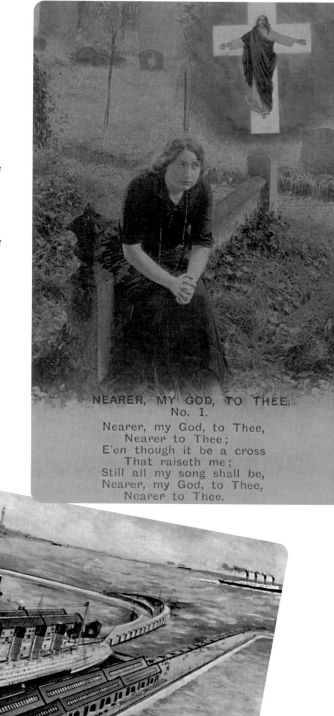

NEARER, MY GOD, TO THEE.
No. 1.
Nearer, my God, to Thee,
Nearer to Thee;
E'en though it be a cross
That raiseth me;
Still all my song shall be,
Nearer, my God, to Thee,
Nearer to Thee.

NEW GLADSTONE DOCKS, LIVERPOOL.

SHOWING CUNARD LINERS IN BERTH

NEARER, MY GOD, TO THEE.
No. 2.

There let my way appear,
Steps unto heaven,
All that Thou sendest me
In mercy given,
Angels to beckon me
Nearer, my God, to Thee,
Nearer to Thee.

NEARER, MY GOD, TO THEE.
No. 3.

Then, with my waking thoughts
Bright with Thy praise,
Out of my stony griefs
Bethel I'll raise;
So by my woes to be
Nearer, my God, to Thee,
Nearer to Thee.   Amen.

R.M.S. Virginian, (Allan Line) 12,000 Tons, Turbine.

Above left: The equipment in ship's Marconi cabin at the time of the *Titanic* disaster.

Below left: A wireless cabin the mid-1920s.

Top: Cunard's *Carpathia* (1902) at Palermo. This is the ship that picked up *Titanic's* survivors from the North Atlantic.

Above: Allan Line advertising card from the early 1900s.

Left: Another Edwardian Allan Line advertising card.

R.M.S. Empress of Ireland

LATE
R.M.S. Alsatian

Length, 600 ft.
Width, 72 ft.
Tonnage, 18,000

R.M.S. EMPRESS of FRANCE.

Above left: In the Canadian Pacific Line's equivalent of the *Titanic* disaster, the *Empress of Ireland* sank in the St Lawrence River following a collision, with the loss of 1,053 lives on 29 May 1914.

Left: Canadian Pacific's *Empress of France* (1913) in her original Allan Line livery as the *Alsatian*.

Above right: In 1919 the Allan liner *Alsatian* was taken over by the Canadian Pacific Line, renamed *Empress of France* and repainted in CPR livery.

Right: Another view of *Aquitania*.

WHITE STAR LINE

R.M.S. "Oceanic" 704 feet long. 17.274 tons.
Services to New York, South Africa,
Australia and New Zealand.
ISMAY, IMRIE & Co. LONDON & LIVERPOOL.

Left: Greetings card claiming to be written on the *Cymric* illustrating the *Oceanic*. *Cymric* was torpedoed and sunk in 1916

Below: Canadian Pacific's *Empress of France* (1913).

R.M.S. Metagama

R.M.S. Minnedosa

Left: Canadian Pacific liner
Left: Canadian Pacific liner *Metagama* (1914), used primarily on the Liverpool to St John's, Newfoundland, route.

Below: Canadian Pacific's *Minnedosa* (1917) served on the Liverpool to Quebec route for most of the 14 years she was with the line. *Minnedosa* was sold to the Italians in 1931 for scrapping but the Italian Government pressed her into service as a troopship.

Continued on page 61.

Cunard's *Aquitania*, *armania*, *Caronia* and *usitania* were requisitioned y the government for war rvice. However, *Lusitania* as quickly returned to unard so that the regular ansatlantic service could be aintained.

Canadian Pacific also played part in the war. The *Empress France* was requisitioned on 6 ugust 1914 and rapidly nverted into an armed merchant uiser by the addition of eight 6in ns. Manned by a Royal Navy ew, the *Empress of France* sailed om Liverpool on 15 August to join the Tenth Cruiser Squadron n duty with the Northern Patrol watching the passage between eland and the Shetlands. In December she was made flagship of e squadron and during her time with Northern Patrol, until early 918, she intercepted 15,000 ships.

The *Empress of Russia* was earmarked for war service while she as still in Vancouver preparing for a voyage to Hong Kong in ugust 1914. On her arrival there her bunker capacity was nlarged and she was fitted with eight 4.7in guns. With a crew of ritish naval reservists and French gunners, *Empress of Russia*

sailed to the Indian Ocean where she met up with the Australian cruiser HMAS *Sydney*. A little while before, the Australian warship had sunk the German cruiser *Emden* and the survivors were put aboard the Canadian Pacific vessel for transportation to Ceylon. The *Empress of Russia* then assisted in the capture of the Turkish fortress at Kamaran on the Red Sea. Later she and the *Empress of Asia* guarded the British outpost of Aden for 23 days until the arrival of Royal Navy vessels. Still later in the war the *Empress of Russia*, *Empress of Asia*, *Empress of Japan*, the cruiser HMS *Himalaya* and the destroyer HMS *Ribble* blockaded the port of Manila where 15 German vessels awaited a chance to slip out and deliver their precious cargoes to the homeland.

Right: Carmania (1905),
another Cunard liner that served
with distinction as an armed
merchant cruiser in World War 1.

Below: Carmania in a colour
card with a Cunard sister ship in
the background.

S. S. Carmania. 20000 Tons. 21000 Horsepower. 650 ft Long, 72 ft. Broad.

The *Empress of Britain* (later renamed *Montroyal*) was also pressed into war service as an armed merchant cruiser in August 1914 and served for a year on South African patrol. Then she was fitted out as a troopship and transported troops to the Dardanelles, India and Egypt. In between these voyages she also carried Canadian troops across the Atlantic to fight in the trenches of the Western Front. During one of these trips from Canada, with 5,000 troops aboard, *Empress of Britain* was attacked by a German U-boat. Fortunately the liner was zigzagging at the time because the attack was not noticed until one torpedo passed 3ft in front of the bow and another about 12ft from the stern.

During the Great War the Norddeutscher Lloyd's *Kaiser Wilhelm der Grosse* was pressed into service as an armed commerce raider by the German Government. On the morning of 26 August 1914 she was found, while coaling from two auxiliary ships, off the mouth of the River Oro in West Africa by the British cruiser HMS *Highflyer*. The German vessel refused to surrender and, after the auxiliaries were allowed to retire to a safe distance, battle commenced. Although armed with only 4.1in guns against the British warship's 6in, the *Kaiser Wilhelm der Grosse* put up a brave fight. However, the outcome was inevitable and after about half an hour the cruiser's heavier weight of fire began to tell. A 6in shell tore a huge hole in the liner's side just on her waterline. Slowly the German ship began to heel over to port and her crew were forced to abandon her. Several boatloads of German sailors were observed leaving the stricken vessel, at which time the British warship ceased fire. A signal was made to the liner to the effect that should the crew wish to abandon ship then the cruiser would not interfere. Two boats with surgeons, medical attendants and stores were lowered from the *Highflyer* to see what they could do for the enemy's wounded. Shortly afterwards the liner sank, but not before almost 400 of her crew had managed to escape to the waiting auxiliary vessels. Only

R. M. S. Caronia (Cunard Line).

"CARONIA."

Above: Caronia[1] in colour. Note how much styles had changed in 40 years by comparing this Caronia with the next picture, Caronia[2].

Right: Cunard's Caronia[2] (1947), demonstrating that change is not necessarily improvement.

Right: A colour card of *Caronia[1]*.

Below: The Canadian Pacific liner *Empress of Britain* (1905) was converted into an armed merchant cruiser during World War 1. She was later renamed *Montroyal*.

R.M.S. Empress of Britain

Right: Lifeboats being lowered from HMS *Highflyer* to go to the aid of the crew of the *Kaiser Wilhelm der Grosse*. The German liner had been operating as a commerce raider when the Royal Navy cruiser caught up with her o the morning of 26 August 1914. The liner refused to surrender and in an unequal gun duel was quickl battered into submission by the British cruiser.

one crewman had been killed on the *Highflyer*, while something like 200 had died aboard the *Kaiser Wilhelm der Grosse*. The escapees were captured a fortnight later when the Hamburg Amerika liner *Bethania* was taken.

On 14 September the *Carmania*, now an armed merchant cruiser, fought and sank the German armed merchantman *Cap Trafalgar*, which had previously been a Hamburg Amerika Line ship, off the South American coast. Like the *Kaiser Wilhelm der Grosse* the *Cap Trafalgar* was coaling when she was found but immediately despatched her auxiliaries and started to steam away from the much slower *Carmania*. However, once it was realised that the *Carmania* was alone, the German ship turned and attacked, and at about 12.10pm the battle began. For some unexplained reason,

the German gunners fired at the superstructure of the British shi while *Carmania's* guns were aimed at the enemy vessel's waterlin Two British shells in rapid succession struck the *Cap Trafalg* forward and steam was seen issuing from ruptured pipes. The shi by this time were less than two miles apart and both were on fir *Cap Trafalgar* was slowly heeling over to starboard but still her gu continued to fire until at about 1.50pm she rolled right over onto he side and sank. *Carmania* was also badly damaged and on fire. On prompt action by the crew of the British ship managed to keep he afloat. The British had lost nine men, while it was estimated that least 250 of the German crew had either been killed in the action had gone down with the ship. *Cap Trafalgar's* colliers had manage to pick 292 German survivors from the sea.

Above and right: On 14 September 1914 the British armed merchant cruiser, *Carmania*, met its German counterpart, *Cap Trafalgar*, in the South Atlantic. Unfortunately for the German ship she was only equipped with 4.1in guns compared to the 6in weapons fitted to the British vessel. However, the German guns were much more modern than the British ones and had a higher rate of fire, so the battle was not quite as one-sided as might be imagined. Before long the *Cap Trafalgar* was on fire and water was gushing into her through the holes in her hull made by British shells. Slowly the *Cap Trafalgar* began to heel over to starboard and sink. The *Carmania* had not escaped unscathed. A shell had set fire to her below the bridge and at the same time severed her fire hose to that area. If the *Cap Trafalgar* had not been already sinking then the battle could well have gone badly for the *Carmania*. Eventually the fires were brought under control and the *Carmania* radioed HMS *Bristol* for assistance. The British ship held her fire as the German auxiliary vessels returned to the rapidly sinking *Cap Trafalgar* and picked up her 292 survivors.

TAKE UP THE SWORD OF JUSTICE

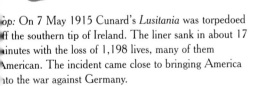

What had appeared to be a helpful gesture on the part of the British Government when it had handed the *Lusitania* back to her owners in 1914 turned into a disaster on 7 May 1915 when the liner was torpedoed off the Old Head of Kinsale at the southern tip of Ireland. *Lusitania* sank in about 17 minutes with the loss of 1,198 lives, many of them Americans. The incident came close to precipitating war between America and Germany (but as the war's final outcome was still unclear the Americans decided to wait a little longer).

Two White Star vessels were lost in 1915. The *Armenian* was torpedoed on 28 June and the *Arabic*[2] on 19 August, both by *U24*.

Also in 1915 it was announced that Canadian Pacific was to absorb the Allan Line and a new company was formed, Canadian Pacific Ocean Services Limited. In reality the line had already been absorbed, as Canadian Pacific had bought all of the capital stock by early September 1909. Why the purchase was kept secret until 1915 has never been revealed. The line continued to operate as an independent unit until 16 July 1917 when it was finally swallowed up by Canadian Pacific.

The Great War had meant the end for the Allan Line. The *Alsatian*, *Calgarian* and *Virginian* became armed merchant cruisers. The *Grampian*, *Corinthian*, *Sicilian*, *Scandinavian*, *Scotian* and *Tunisian* were taken over as troopships and carried the Canadian

Top: On 7 May 1915 Cunard's *Lusitania* was torpedoed off the southern tip of Ireland. The liner sank in about 17 minutes with the loss of 1,198 lives, many of them American. The incident came close to bringing America into the war against Germany.

Top right: An allied attempt to bring America into the Great War soon after the sinking of the *Lusitania*.

Above: Survivors from the *Lusitania* being picked up from the sea.

CUNARD R.M.S. "ROYAL GEORGE" AT QUEBEC.

Expeditionary Force across the Atlantic. The *Livonian*, *Numidian* and *Mongolian* were taken over by the Admiralty and the first two were sunk as blockships. *Mongolian* was torpedoed and sunk off Filey Brigg, Yorkshire, in 1918.

In November 1916 the last of the 'Olympic' class ships, *Britannic*, which had been completed as a hospital ship, struck a mine in the Aegean Sea and sank 50 minutes later. Fortunately the ship was not carrying wounded servicemen at the time. Crew and medical staff successfully made it into the lifeboats. Unfortunately, Captain Bartlett thought that he could move his damaged ship into shallow water and perhaps beach her. He failed but in the attempt, with the ship sinking by the bows and lifting her propellers out of the water, the revolving screws drew in a couple of the boats and chewed them and their occupants to pieces; 21 people were killed and another 28 were seriously injured.

Cunard's new headquarters building at Liverpool's pierhead was completed in 1917. The building still stands although the Cunard Line is but a shadow of its former self.

In January 1917 White Star's *Laurentic* struck a mine and sank off Malin Head on the northern tip of Ireland, while transporting £5 million worth of gold bullion. The Admiralty later recovered 95% of the lost gold.

In April 1917 the *Justicia* was completed as a troopship by Harland & Wolff. The vessel had originally been intended for the Holland America Line as the *Statendam*, the second of that name

for the compan until the British Government to her over. *Justicia* had been so named because she wa supposedly going to be manned by the surviving crew fro Cunard's *Lusitania*. However, *Lusitania*'s crew had been disperse by the time *Justicia* was ready but the crew from *Britannic*[2] we still together so the ship was passed to White Star. *Britannic*'s cre were not the luckiest group ever assembled, even if they thoug they were when the new, large and elegant *Justicia* was handed ove to them. Just after 2.00pm on Friday, 19 July 1918, about 20 mile from the Hebrides, *Justicia* was struck by a single torpedo fro *UB64*. The engine room was flooded and the ship was helpless b in no immediate danger of sinking. At 4.30 two more torpedoe were spotted racing toward the seemingly helpless liner. On torpedo missed and the other was destroyed by gunfire fro *Justicia*'s crew. By 8.00pm *Justicia* was under tow towards Loug Swilly when yet another torpedo was seen coming towards he Again, gunfire from the liner averted disaster as the torpedo wa driven off course. Another attack came at 4.30 the followin morning when a torpedo was seen passing a short distance ahea of the ship. The final blow fell at 9.30am and came from *U54* which fired a salvo of torpedoes at the liner's port quarter. Tw torpedoes found their target and *Justicia* began to settle deeper i the water. The ship was finally abandoned before she sank short after 12.30. The only casualties from *Justicia*, despite th determined attacks by German U-boats, were the third enginee and 15 ratings, all killed by the very first torpedo. The German had not fared too well either and *UB124* had been sunk by one o *Justicia*'s escorts, HMS *Marne*.

White Star's *Southland* was torpedoed and sunk on 4 Jun

Left: Cunard's *Royal George* (1916) which worked on the Liverpool to New York route. The ship was so badly stabilised that she was known to her crew as 'Rolling George'.

Right: White Star's *Regina* (1917), which began life as a troopship, became a regular transatlantic liner after World War 1, plying back and forth between Liverpool and New York.

Below right: Aquitania (1914) menu for a special British Peace Day dinner aboard ship on 19 July 1919.

1918 about 140 miles off Northern Ireland. *Delphic* was torpedoed and sunk about 135 miles southwest of the Scillies on 20 July.

In 1918 Canadian Pacific's *Empress of France* transferred to Atlantic convoy escort duties. From then until the end of the war she escorted nine convoys of about 20 ships each, carrying some 30,000 troops. Throughout her war service *Empress of France* steamed more than a quarter of a million nautical miles.

During the hostilities Canadian Pacific lost 13 vessels to enemy action, among them the *Calgarian*. During her early war service *Calgarian*, with HMS *Vindictive*, blockaded the port of Lisbon, bottling up potential German raiders lurking there. Then she was employed patrolling the Atlantic trade routes. Later still she was attached to the North America and West Indies Station, patrolling off New York. In March 1918, while escorting a convoy of 30 ships bound for Britain, *Calgarian* was struck by four torpedoes and sank with the loss of 49 lives. Despite everything, between August 1914 and October 1919 Canadian Pacific vessels transported over a million troops, many thousands of horses and mules and over four million tons of cargo and munitions.

During the war the Cunard Line lost a total of 22 ships. At least some of these vessels had to be replaced and as soon as it possibly could Cunard ordered 13 new ships, then the single largest order ever from a single company.

Cunard Line

Peace 1919

BRITISH PEACE DAY.

DINNER

Hors d'Œuvres—Americaine

Consomme George V   Potage President Wilson

Supremes de Turbotin—Liberte

Noisettes d'Agneau—Clemenceau

Roast Sirloins—John Bull

Haricot Verts—Francaise

Pommes Nouvelles

Long Island Duckling
Salade Liggett

Pouding Belgique
Poires—Dame Paix

Dessert

R.M.S. "AQUITANIA."

SATURDAY, JULY 19, 1919

THE GOLDEN AGE

In 1918 the Japanese Toyo Kisen Line was formed, and with its three crack liners presented Canadian Pacific with some serious competition on the Pacific routes. To overcome this problem Canadian Pacific ordered two new three-funnel liners, the *Empress of Russia*[2] and the *Empress of China*[2], which would be considerably faster than the Japanese vessels. To drive home its point Canadian Pacific also acquired the magnificent *Empress of Scotland*, the line's largest and most luxurious vessel to date. At 25,000 gross register tons the *Empress of Scotland* was also the largest liner on the Canadian run. All of these vessels operated on Atlantic routes from time to time.

During the interwar period Canadian Pacific operated several more notable vessels on the North Atlantic. With others occasionally brought in from Pacific service, the regular Atlantic service was maintained by the *Empress of France* at 18,400 tons, *Montlaurier* of 17,000 tons, *Montcalm*, *Montclare*, and *Montrose*, each of 16,400 tons, *Montroyal* of 15,850 tons, *Minnedosa* and *Melita* of 14,000 tons each, and *Metagama* of 12,450 tons. *Empress of France* set a new record time for the passage from Liverpool to Quebec in 1920. In 1921 the Canadian Pacific Railroad Company changed its name for the operation of vessels on the North Atlantic to Canadian Pacific Steamships Ltd. In 1922 the Canadian Pacific line temporarily moved its British base of operations to Southampton but the *Montcalm*, *Montrose* and *Montclare* continued to operate the Liverpool to Canada service.

During World War 1 White Star had lost 10 ships, and in the year following its vessels were beset by a spate of fires and collisions. In December 1918 an explosion in *Adriatic's* engine room put the ship out of action for two days. In just over a month, in May and June 1919, shortly after leaving New York, the same vessel caught fire twice. In late July *Cedric* suffered a serious fire while still at her New York berth and in September *Vedic* went aground in the Orkney Islands. Then in late November, shortly after leaving New York harbour, *Adriatic* collided with the British steamer *St Michael*.

IMM had never been the financial success that J. P. Morgan had

envisaged, so in 1919 the company decided to dispose of White Star and the rest of its British shipping interests for the n[ot] unreasonable sum of £27 million. A British consortium headed b[y] Lord Pirrie of Harland & Wolff and Owen Phillips (later [to] become Lord Kylsant) supremo of the Royal Mail Line sought [to] make the purchase but the plan was vetoed by no less a person tha[n] President Woodrow Wilson himself. Unable to unload White Sta[r] IMM took the alternative route and continued to expand it. *Bardi[c]* *Gallic*, *Canopic* and *Cretic*, as the best available wartime-bui[lt] vessels, were brought in.

Olympic, which had been refitted and converted to oil burnin[g] after her war duties, re-entered White Star service in mid-summe[r] 1920 and *Lapland* was temporarily handed back t[o] Red Star. The following year *Belgic*[4] was als[o] returned to Red Star service as *Belgenland*. A[s] war reparation White Star Line had been given among others, the German liner *Berlin*, an[d] renamed her *Arabic*[3] to help make up th[e] numbers. Unhappily, the number of ships was n[ot] that important as the American Governmen[t] introduced what was known as the 'Three Percen[t] Act' which limited the number of immigrants to th[e] country to 360,000 for three years.

In 1921 the new *Albania*[2] entered Cunar[d] service, along with the slightly smaller *Scythia*[2] and *Samaria*[2]. The following year the *Laconia*[2] *Lancastria*, *Andania*[2], *Antonia*[2] and *Ausonia*[2] joined the fleet. Over the next three years the *Franconia*[3] *Aurania*[3], *Ascania*[2], *Alaunia*[2] and *Carinthia*[2] joined bringing the fleet up to an acceptable level.

The Royal Mail Line had been founded in 184[0] and, with a then enormous fleet of 14 steamers, carried transatlanti[c] mail to the West Indies and South America. Although it was thus [a] long-established concern, the Royal Mail Line started carryin[g] transatlantic passengers only in 1921, from Hamburg to New Yor[k] via Southampton. Initially the line managed with just three liners bu[t] this was soon increased to five.

By 1922 the Leyland Line, another member of the IM[M] group, was so short of ships that the cattle boat *Bovic* was hande[d] over to it, becoming the *Colonian*. Another war reparations vessel the Norddeutscher Lloyd liner *Columbus* then became White Star'[s] *Homeric*. Three more first-class vessels were handed over by th[e]

Continued on page 78.

72

WILLS'S CIGARETTES

S.S. CONTE ROSSO.

WILLS'S CIGARETTES.

S.S. EMPRESS

WILLS'S CIGARETTES

S.S. NALDERA.

WILLS'S CIGARETTES.

S.S. RESOLUTE.

WILLS'S CIGARETTES.

R.M.S. FRANCONIA

WILLS'S CIGARETTES.

S.S. AMERICA.

WILLS'S CIGARETTES.

R.M.S. SCYTHIA.

WILLS'S CIGARETTES.

S.S. LEVIATHAN.

WILLS'S CIGARETTES.

S.S. MONTROSE.

WILLS'S CIGARETTES.

WILLS'S CIGARETTES.

T.S.S. BALTIC.

LLS'S CIGARETTES.

S.S. CEDRIC.

WILLS'S CIGARETTES.

S.S. MAJESTIC.

S.S. BELGENLAND.

Collecting cigarette cards was
a popular hobby between the
wars and the liners were a
favourite subject.

LE HAVRE . *Paquebot "Paris"*

Ligne du Havre à New York, 233 m. de long, 26 m. de large, jauge 37.000 tonnes, 664 homme d'équipage, 98 passagers de luxe, 468 passagers de 1ᵉ classe, 464 passagers de 2ᵉ classe, 2210 passagers de 3ᵉ classe, soit un total de 3.210 passagers.

Left: The French liner *Paris* (1921), belonging to the Compagnie Generale Transatlantique. In 1939 the *Paris* caught fire and sank at her berth in Le Havre.

Below: Standard badges of rank and department used by the mercantile marine.

MERCANTILE MARINE STANDARD UNIFORM

DISTINCTIONS OF RANK, ETC.

Key to Coloured Plate

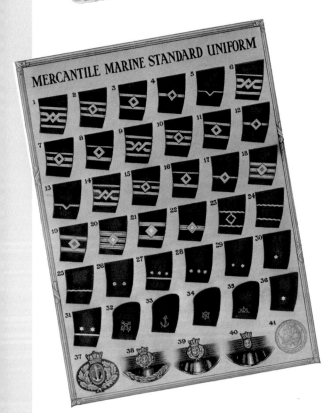

1. Certificated Master.
2.   ,,   Chief Officer.
3.   ,,   Second Officer.
4.   ,,   Third and Junior Certificated Officers.
5. Uncertificated Junior Officer.
6. Second Master.
7. First Officer.
8. Junior Second Officer.
9. Certificated Chief Engineer. All Engineer officers wear *purple* insertion.
10.   ,,   Second Engineer and Chief Refrigerating Engineer.
11.   ,,   Third Engineer and Second Refrigerating Engineer.
12.   ,,   Fourth and Junior Engineers.
13. Uncertificated Junior Engineers, Refrigerating Engineers, Boilermakers and Electricians.
14. Second Chief Engineer.
15. Junior Second Engineer.
16. Junior Third Engineer.
17. Junior Fourth Engineer.
18. Ship Surgeon. All Medical Officers wear *scarlet* insertion.
19.   ,,   ,,   Assistant.
20. Senior Purser, where three or more are carried.   Pursers wear *white* insertion.
21. Purser.
22.   ,,   Assistant.
23. First Wireless Operator.
24. Second Wireless Operator.
25. Third Wireless Operator.
26. Cadets or Apprentices.
27. Chief Steward on Passenger Vessels.
28. Assistant Chief Steward.
29. Steward.
30. Assistant Steward.
31. Steward on Cargo Vessels.
32. Boatswain.
33. Boatswain's Mate.
34. Quartermaster.
35. Quartermaster's Mate.
36. Cook.
37. Standard Cap Badge for Officers.
38. Peak of Master's Cap.
39. Peak of Cap for all other Officers.
40. Petty Officers' Cap Badge.
41. Mercantile Marine Coat Button.

R.M.S. "Empress of France."
Length, 600 ft.
Breadth, 72 ft.
Tonnage, 18,000.

GROSS TONNAGE 16,418

CANADIAN PACIFIC S.S. "MONTCALM"

CANADIAN PACIFIC S. S. "MONTCLARE"   Gross Tonnage 16,314

Top: Canadian Pacific's *Empress of France* in the 1920s.

Above: The Canadian Pacific liner *Montcalm* (1922) in the River Mersey in the 1920s.

Left: Canadian Pacific's *Montclare* (1922), sister ship to *Montcalm* and *Montrose*. The ships operated the Liverpool to Canada service.

Canadian Pacific S.S. MONTROSE. gross tonnage

Left: Canadian
Pacific's *Montrose*
(1922).

Right: Tranatlantic Liners with
their vast coal burning
consumption were serviced pre
WW1 mainly by colliers such as
this one at Liverpool circa 1911.

Below: The Cunard liner *Scythia*.

A COLLIER DISCHARGING

Cunard White Star   "Scythia"

Left: A boiler room on Cunard's *Aquitania* before her conversion to oil fuel in 1919.

Below: The same boiler room on *Aquitania* after her conversion to oil.

Left: Cunard's *Samaria*[2], which usually sailed between Liverpool and Boston.

R.M.S. SAMARIA.

Right: The Cunard liner *Tyrrhenia* (1922), which was renamed *Lancastria* in 1924.

Below: Lancastria, formerly the *Tyrrhenia,* which was bombed by German aircraft while evacuating women, children and British troops from St Nazaire in France on 16 June 1940. More than 3,000 passengers and crew were killed.

CUNARD LINE   THE NEW OIL-BURNING LINER "TYRRHENIA"   GROSS TONNAGE 17,000

Cunard White Star   *Lancastria*

Germans. They were the Hamburg Amerika Line's *Imperator,* *Vaterland* and the incomplete *Bismarck. Vaterland* went to the American Line and became *Leviathan. Imperator* went to Cunard and became *Berengaria,* where in company with the *Mauretania* and *Aquitania* she would be used to open up a new route between Southampton and New York in place of the old Liverpool to New York run. *Bismarck,* the largest ship in the world, became White Star's *Majestic[2].* The American Line, somewhat mendaciously, claimed that its *Leviathan* was the largest ship but *Majestic* was 6ft longer and 2,918grt larger.

It was not only ships that were leaving a defeated Germany. Hordes of Germans were emigrating to America, and to cater for this exodus *Vedic* and the Red Star Line's *Poland* operated an emigrant service out of Bremen. For this service *Poland* was decked out in White

Star livery. On the Canadian route the new *Doric[2],* which joined the line in 1923, shared the trade with the Dominion Line's *Regina.*

In the twenties Cunard and White Star vied with one another to win the patronage of celebrity passengers such as Mary Pickford, Douglas Fairbanks senior and junior, and the odd racehorse such as Papyrus who was provided with his own specially constructed cabin aboard *Aquitania* in 1923. In one week of October that year, White Star transported Dame Nellie Melba, Dame Clara Butt, Anna Pavlova, and the Prince of Wales across the Atlantic. Captains of the liners, particularly during the interwar years, pandered to every whim of their more famous passengers. The line that attracted the most celebrities could rely on many more ordinary first class bookings from mere mortals wishing to bathe in the stars' reflected glory, so the practices were encouraged by the owners.

In 1924, while on an inspection tour of South American ports, Lord Pirrie, the head of Harland & Wolff, collapsed and died. That left the way clear for Lord Kylsant to take over the Belfast shipyard. Kylsant had been interested in taking over White Star ever since the line had first been offered for sale in 1919. Now as the line's preferred builder he took an even keener interest. Then in 1924 White Star gave Harland & Wolff notice that the 'cost plus profit' basis under which all its vessels had been built was to come to an end. The following year, IMM let it be known that it was again interested in selling off its British shipping interests, just as it had seven years earlier. There was an obvious solution to the problem. Kylsant would buy White Star. *Continued on page 84*

Above: Cunard's *Laconia*[2] (1922). *Laconia* was torpedoed off the coast of West Africa in 1942 while carrying more than 1,800 Italian prisoners of war.

Left: Another view of the *Laconia*.

Below: The Cunard liner *Antonia* (1922).

Left: Cunard's *Andania*^{2} (1922).

Below left: The Cunard Line's *Ausoni...* (1922).

Below: A colour card showing Cunard's *Andania*^{2} at sea. *Andania* was torpedoed and sunk in 1940.

Right: Cunard's *Franconia*^{2} (1923).

Below right: A dramatic 1920s Cunar... advertising card.

FASTEST OCEAN SERVICE IN THE WORLD

CUNARD

SOUTHAMPTON, CHERBOURG AND NEW YORK

R.M.S. "MAURETANIA"   R.M.S. "BERENGARIA"   R.M.S. "AQUITANIA"

White Star Line, R.M.S. "Homeric" 34,351 Tons

Above left: The American liner *Leviathan*, formerly the
German *Vaterland*, entering her New York berth. The
Americans mendaciously claimed this vessel as the
world's largest liner but in reality White Star's *Majestic*[2]
was not only 6ft longer but 2,918 gross register tons
larger.

Left: The White Star liner *Homeric* in the 1920s.

Above: The Pacific Steam Navigation liner *Orbita* in the
1920s. Despite the company name, the line was formed
in 1868 to provide a transatlantic service.

Above right: A 1925 White Star Line advertisement.

Right: The Royal Mail Steam Packet liner *Araguaya* in
the 1920s.

S.S. SPHINX
Compagnie des Messageries Maritimes

Left: A 1920s view of the French liner *Sphinx*

Right: A 1920s' White Star advertisement for *Majestic[2]*.

Below: Another White Star Line advertisement from the 1920s, showing the line's main services. The vessel is White Star's most successful liner, *Olympic*.

WHITE STAR LINE

TO
U.S.A
CANADA
SOUTH AFRICA
AUSTRALIA & NEW ZEALAND

THE "BIG SHIP" ROUTE

Whatever its ownership, White Star desperately needed new ships if its reputation was to be maintained, so the *Laurentic[2]* was ordered from Harland & Wolff, but not on the old 'cost plus' basis. To save money the new ship was to be built as cheaply as possible, even to being coal fired. The cost-cutting exercise was a miserable failure. The ship, which entered service in 1927, was not liked by transatlantic travellers.

Late in 1926 Kylsant made an offer of £7 million for White Star, rather more than the company was worth, which was accepted. On 1 January 1927 White Star Line Ltd was formed to take over the Royal Mail Line's shares in White Star's parent company Oceanic Steam Navigation. There was only one major fly in the ointment. Kylsant did not have the money to run the line, so, keeping with the line's established character, he resorted to a few sharp practices of his own. Although the Royal Mail Line was large — the group owned the world's largest fleet of ships at one time — it had expanded far too quickly under Kylsant's management. The situation was not helped by Kylsant's formation of the Aberdeen & Commonwealth Line using White Star Line resources and his added purchase of the Shaw Savill & Albion Line. By the late 1920s the Royal Mail Line was in serious financial trouble and owed a lot of money to the British Treasury, and the loans were fast becoming due for repayment.

Many of the Royal Mail and White Star ships

were getting a bit long in the tooth but the Kylsant group simply did not have the cash on hand to replace them. In 1928 White Star's *Medic*, *Athenic* and *Suevic* were all sold off and not replaced. The new *Oceanic*[3], intended to replace *Homeric*, was cancelled even though construction had begun. Following the take-over, the Royal Mail Line service between Southampton and New York was discontinued and the business taken on by White Star. *Ohio* and *Orca* were passed to White Star service as *Albertic* and *Calgaric* but the ageing *Persic* was sold off for scrap and not replaced. Things went from bad to worse for the company when, on 10 December 1928, the *Celtic* was wrecked at the entrance to Queenstown harbour. The following year a second instalment on the Royal Mail Group's treasury loan became due but the company was unable to pay it.

In an attempt to raise a little cash Kylsant's company invited the public to subscribe to a £2 million debenture issue, promising that the company was trading at a healthy profit when in reality there was no profit at all. The deception was obvious and the company's financial manoeuvrings came under investigation. The major part of the investigation into the Royal Mail group's financial dealings was completed in 1930 with the result that Kylsant was removed as the head of the company and given a leave of absence from which he would never return. In September of the following year he was arrested for issuing false reports for 1926 and 1927 and jailed for his part in the swindle. He served one year. To his credit he accepted full responsibility for the affair and was the only director of Royal Mail to be severely punished.

Continued on page 96.

WHITE STAR LINE

To UNITED STATES CANADA SOUTH AFRICA AUSTRALIA *and* NEW ZEALAND

White Star Line Agency—
R. ECCLESTON,
17, Rainhall Road,
BARNOLDSWICK.

Canadian Pacific Liner Empress of France, 20,400.

Above: White Star advertisement, this time showing *Majestic*[2].

Left: The Canadian Pacific liner *Empress of France*[2], until 1947 the same line's *Duchess of Bedford* (1928).

Above right: The Canadian Pacific liner *Duchess of Bedford* (1928) was renamed *Empress of France*[2] in 1948 and sailed on under that name until 1960.

Right: Canadian Pacific's *Duchess of Richmond* (1929), here seen before she was subsequently renamed *Empress of Canada*.

Canadian Pacific Liner Empress of France, 20,000 tons

HANDS OVER SEA

The transatlantic liner trade was based on the vast numbers of Europeans who crossed the Atlantic to begin new lives in the United States of America. Many of these people left families and loved ones behind. The need for these people to keep in touch with one another was clearly seen by the various shipping lines who produced 'Hands Across The Sea' cards to capitalise on that need.

From Across the Sea

Best of wishes
I now send,
Though face
to face
we cannot stand,
Just to tell you
my dear Friend
I fain would
grip and
shake your
hand

WALTER BALFOUR.

A MERRY CHRISTMAS.

Now distance
doth divide us,
And I'm far
across the sea
I wonder, yes I wonder,
do you sometimes
think of me?

On rapid wing
o'er Land and Sea,
My message speeds its flight
to thee.

PAST GOLDEN MEMORIES.

PRESENT. HAPPY DAYS.

FUTURE THAT YOU'LL REMEMBER ME.

HANDS ACROSS THE SEA

Here's a wish from me,
True as wish can be,
Though the seas divide us
"Hands across the Sea."

HANDS ACROSS THE SEA

What happier greeting can there be,
Whatever may befall,
"Clasp hands with me across the sea,"
And God be with us all.

TO THE ABSENT ONE

HANDS ACROSS THE SEA,
. . . HOW SWEET
THAT WE CAN IN SPIRIT MEET,
EACH TO EACH DEAR FRIEND
. . . SHALL SAY,
JOY TO YOU FROM FAR AWAY.

HANDS ACROSS THE SEA

What happier greeting can there be,
Whatever may befall,
"Clasp hands with me, across the sea"
And God be with us all.

A LINK TO BIND
WHERE CIRCUMSTANCES PART

CHRISTMAS GREETINGS

A VERY HAPPY BIRTHDAY

Over the mighty world of foam,
Take just a wish, from me and home,
All that my heart and lips would say
If I could clasp your hand to-day.

HANDS ACROSS THE SEA.

HANDS ACROSS THE SEA.

In thought I clasp your hand to-day, while wishes for your weal
Spring gaily forth and speed away, and distant friendships seal.

HOMELAND HEART ECHOE

Oh what do I care though
distance will
to sever our hearts fond and
It will not break love's
though for years imu
In the dear Homelan
fr

HANDS ACROSS THE SEA

TO WISH YOU
ALL PROSPERITY

HANDS ACROSS THE SEA.

Love, like a good ship flying free,
Carries our thoughts across the sea;
Whispers of happy days of yore,
Longing to clasp your hand once more.
C.B.

Homeland Echoes o'er the Sea.

SINCE I CANNOT MEET YOU,
AS IN OTHER DAYS,
HERE'S A CARD TO GREET YOU,
JOY BE YOURS ALWAYS.

In 1930, for the first time in its history, the White Star Line failed to make a profit. The *Runic* was sold off and not replaced. *Britannic³* entered service on the Liverpool to New York route, but it was too late for White Star. In 1931 the Kylsant group collapsed and the companies forming it went their separate ways. *Corinthic* and *Arabic³* went to the breaker's yard but White Star struggled on. Then, in 1932, the Australian Government demanded payment on a debt owed; the *Cedric* and *Cufic* were scrapped and not replaced; and the line again traded at a loss. The only bright point was the arrival of the new *Georgic²*, the very last ship built for White Star. The end for the line as an entity in its own right came the next year when the majority of the fleet was sold off. *Baltic*, *Megantic* and *Tropic* went to the breakers. *Gallic* and *Delphic*, cargo vessels, were sold to the Clan Line. *Albertic* and *Calgaric* were laid up while their fate was decided. The White Star Line was bankrupt.

In 1933, the Royal Mail Line's creditors foreclosed (t Australian Government was owed a cool £1 million) with the res that its ships too were hurriedly sold off to offset the debts. Kylsa White Star Company was compulsorily wound up in 1935, owi more than £11 million.

In 1929, the Norddeutscher Lloyd's new *Bremen* had snatch the Blue Riband from *Mauretania*, which had held it for the last : years. Cunard was not unduly worried as it had already beg designing the next generation of super-liners for the Atlantic.

In December 1930 the keel of the first of these new vesse Number 534, *Queen Mary*, was laid at John Brown's Clyde shipya The Cunard Line was, however, in serious trouble, although w nothing like the problems that beset White Star. It was the middle the Great Depression and it could not afford to complete the buildi of its new ship. Fortunately the new Cunard giant had caught t public's imagination, so the British Governme stepped in and advanced the cash to complete her ar a sister ship, but only on the condition that the Cuna and White Star Lines were merged into one. T amalgamation was completed in 1934 and t company became Cunard White Star Ltd and wo restarted on the *Queen Mary*. The White Star Li brought *Majestic²*, *Olympic*, *Homeric*, *Britannic Georgic²*, *Laurentic²*, *Adriatic²* and *Doric²* to t partnership, though *Adriatic* was scrapped within t year. The remaining White Star vessels wou continue to sail under their old flag and in their o livery. In November of the same year the *Queen Ma* was launched.

Above: Most liners had their own small musical company in the 1920s but the Royal Mail Line was unusual in providing this jazz band.

Right: The Dutch liner *Christian Huygens* in the 1920s

It was clearly Cunard's intention to dispose of its old rivals once and for all now that it had control. Of the new company's 10 directors six were Cunard men while the remaining four were expected to protect White Star interests — a hopeless task. In 1935 *Olympic* was withdrawn and *Doric*[2] was sent to the breakers. The following year *Majestic*[2] was sold off as a cadet ship and *Homeric* was sent for scrapping.

The *Empress of Britain*, the Canadian Pacific Line's largest vessel on the Southampton to Canada route, collided with the *Briarwood* in 1932 and the *Zafiristan*, in the St Lawrence River, three years later.

In 1935 the French Line's *Normandie* came into service and quickly took the Blue Riband from the *Bremen*. No first class liners ever officially set out to take the Blue Riband, which would have seemed to be 'bad taste' at the time. However, as soon as *Normandie* did take the record, little commemorative medals, complete with blue ribbons, were produced from somewhere and handed out to the passengers. There were just enough to go around. A blue pennant, 30ft long (the ship had made the crossing at 30 knots) also appeared.

continued on page 106.

CUNARD R.M.S. SAMARIA   19,848 TONS.

Greetings and Best Wishes

Top: Cunard's *Samaria*[2] (1921).

Above: The Cunard liner *Aurania*[2] (1924) in the River Mersey.

Left: A 1920s souvenir card from Cunard's *Berengaria* (1921) symbolising the reliability of communication by that time.

Left: Cunard's *Carinthia²* (1924) in unusual livery. *Carinthia²* was sunk by a German U-boat in 1940.

Below left: The French liner *Île de France* (1927) on her maiden voyage from Le Havre to New York. A very long-lived vessel, the *Île de France* survived until 1958, undergoing many changes along the way.

Above: Lifeboat drill aboard Cunard's *Aquitania*.

Above right: One of *Aquitania's* lifeboats in the water during a 1920s boat drill.

Right: Fashion for ships' officers changed over the period from the earliest days of the liners in the 1840 to about 1930 as can be seen in this illustration.

Right: After serving as a troopship during World War 2 the *Île de France* was refitted and converted into a two-funnel ship before being returned to transatlantic service.

Below: Norddeutscher Lloyd's *Bremen* (1929) caught fire and burned out at her berth in 1941.

"BREMEN."

Right: The Norddeutscher Lloyd liner *Europa* (1929). This ship had a very chequered career. She was converted into a troopship in 1940 specifically to bring German soldiers across the English Channel for the planned invasion of Britain. When that enterprise fell through the *Europa* served as a general troopship. At the end of World War 2 she was taken over by the Americans, who also used her as a troopship for repatriating their armies from Europe. Then, in 1946, *Europa* was taken over by the French Line and renamed *Liberté*. The *Liberté* then served on the North Atlantic until 1961, when she was finally sent for scrap.

Above: The Royal Mail liner *Asturias*.

Left and below: In the 1930s White Star introduced the package holiday concept to the North Atlantic liners.

GOOD REASONS

FOR TAKING A

WHITE STAR ☆

☆ ATLANTIC HOLIDAY

1. **HEALTH** : Sea air, sunshine, exercise, relaxation ; both your mind and body will respond to this fourfold tonic.
2. **ADVENTURE** : You will get away from the known and prosaic ; to new scenery, new cities and new customs.
3. **COMFORT** : All the burden of travel is lifted from you ; you simply enjoy the best of everything ashore and afloat without worry.
4. **FRIENDSHIP** : Even if you have not friends or relations to visit on the other side, you will have every opportunity to form new friendships during the tour.
5. **EDUCATION** : No-one is so well educated that he or she will not benefit by travelling abroad. This tour will broaden your whole outlook on life.
6. **PROFIT** : Whatever your occupation, you will find it an interesting contrast to " see how they do it over there " ; you will learn something yourself.
7. **ECONOMY** : Your return ocean fare need not cost you more than

£38 : 0 : 0 or £52 : 15 : 0

TOURIST THIRD CABIN   CABIN

PERSONALLY CONDUCTED TOURS

"ALL-IN" PRICE *from*   NEW YORK

QUEBEC   £58 : 10 : 0   BOSTON

OTTAWA

including Tourist Third Cabin Ocean Fare

MONTREAL   TORONTO

NIAGARA FALLS

OTHER INLAND TOURS CAN BE ARRAN
FROM £7 IN ADDITION TO THE OCEAN

WHITE STAR LI

ATLANTIC HOLIDAYS ☆

FROM £38 RETURN OCEAN FARE

WHITE STAR

CANADIAN PACIFIC S.S. "EMPRESS OF BRITAIN."   GROSS TONNAGE 42,500

Left: Canadian Pacific's *Empress of Britain* (1930) gained the dubious distinctio of being the largest liner sun during World War 2 when a German U-boat and aircraft destroyed her in 1940, with the loss of 45 lives.

Below: A menu cover for a Carnival dinner aboard the Canadian Pacific's *Montcalm* on 7 August 1933.

Right: The front page of a newspaper from the Canadia Pacific liner *Empress of Britain*. First class liners produced their own newspapers while they were at sea.

CANADIAN PACIFIC STEAMSHIP LINES

Music Programme.

Selection

Fox Trot

Savoy Scottish Medley

Cavalcade

Stormy Weather

...   ...

Coward

Koehler

arr. Somers

CROWS NEST

Canadian Pacific

Empress of Britain
World Cruise News

Day No. 20	Tuesday, January 29, 1935	Issue No. 12

TRADE COMMISSION AND UTILITY COMPANIES

DRASTIC ACTION URGED

WASHINGTON.—Drastic Federal legislation to curb the might of giant Utility holding companies through stern taxation measures and criminal statutes was recommended to the Senate on Sunday by the Federal Trade Commission in its final report on a six year investigation of gas and electric Utilities.

The Commission asserted that stringent measures were needed to protect the rate paying public and stock investors from the alleged evils of the holding company system, which, it is charged, is threatening to become a monopoly through the laxity of State laws.

PRINCE NAPOLEON'S PROCLAMATION

PARIS.— From his exile in Switzerland, Prince Napoleon, 21 year old pretender to the throne of the "French Empire," addressed a proclamation to "his people" on Sunday. He pleaded for another Napoleonic regime.

It was read by Prince Joachim Murat, his cousin, at a mass meeting held to launch the young Prince on his political career three days after his coming of age, and to make his name a definite factor in French politics.

SANTIAGO, Chile.—A record heat wave afflicted central Chile on Saturday, the temperature reaching 111 degrees at Chillan.

EMPIRE AIR SERVICES DEVELOPMENT

DEPARTURE OF DELEGATION

LONDON.—According to the *Daily Telegraph* the acceleration and development of the Empire air services is being brought nearer by the departure to India, Siam, Singapore, and Australia of a delegation from the Air Ministry and the Post Office on Tuesday.

The delegates, who are travelling by Imperial Airways, will discuss with local experts ground organisation, including wireless services, night flying, beacons and landing guides, and the co-ordination of the Empire air network.

The full scheme will occupy two years of preparation, meanwhile the aircraft types envisaged will be approved and produced.

PARLIAMENT RE-ASSEMBLING

LONDON.—Parliament reassembles on Monday after the Christmas recess. The new Bills which the Government hope to pass during the session are :—1. Housing Bills for England & Scotland to deal with overcrowding. 2. A Bill to provide for the reorganisation of the Herring Industry. 3. A measure to extend Unemployment Insurance to Agricultural Workers.

The second reading of the Indian Constitutional Reform Bill this week is expected to cause a heated debate.

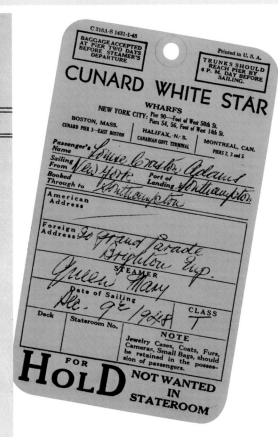

Above: Baggage Label circa 1948

Below: S. S. *Doric*[2], 1922, scrapped in1935 following collision with Formigny.

Right: White Star's *Britannic*³ (1930) in the River Mersey on her first voyage.

Below: A colour view of White Star's *Britannic*³.

C. R. Hoffmann
Southampton. 1246

CUNARD WHITE STAR M.V. "BRITANNIC.
One of Britains Largest and Fastest Motor Vessels.

27,000 tons

White Star Line

M.V. Britannic

Below: Following the 1934 merger between Cunard and White Star the line advertised itself as Cunard White Star.

America this year by R.M.S. "Queen Mary"

Cunard White Star

Left: The French liner *Normandie* at New York in 1935.

Cunard R.M.S "Queen Mary"

Above: Cunard White Star's *Queen Mary.*

Below: Full side view of the French liner *Normandie* at Le Havre, showing her classic lines.

Left and below left: Cunard White Star's *Mauretania*[2] (1938).

May 1936 saw the maiden voyage of the *Queen Mary* and six months later the keel of her even larger sister ship, *Queen Elizabeth*, was laid at John Brown's yard. Two years later the *Mauretania*[2] and the *Queen Elizabeth* both went down the slipways. Before *Queen Elizabeth* could be completed World War 2 broke out.

On 17 October 1937 Joseph Bruce Ismay died at his home in London. Two years later his father's old company, Oceanic Steam Navigation, was dissolved. By the autumn of 1939 when World War 2 began there were only three White Star Line ships remaining: *Britannic*[3], *Georgic*[2] and *Laurentic*[2]. All were taken over by the British Government for war service, *Laurentic* as an armed merchant cruiser. She was torpedoed and sunk by *U99* in November 1940. *Georgic* was bombed and severely damaged while in the Suez Canal in July 1941. *Georgic* should have been finished but despite all the odds she was towed to India where local craftsmen made her seaworthy. She even managed to carry a cargo on her return voyage to Britain where she would be rebuilt. *Georgic* was out of service for three and a half years so extensive was her damage. By the time she did return, she was hardly recognisable having had one of her two squat funnels removed.

R.M.S. QUEEN MARY

WHITE STAR M.V. "BRITANNIC" AT LIVERPOOL.
THE LARGEST MOTOR SHIP IN THE WORLD.

Top: Cunard White Star's *Queen Mary* (1934).

Above: The Cunard White Star liner *Queen Elizabeth* (1940) at sea.

Right: White Star's *Britannic*[3] (1930) at Liverpool.

Right: The White Star liner *Georgic*[2] (1931) could never be described as beautiful, and the removal of one funnel in 1944 did little to improve her appearance.

Below: A Zeppelin airship flies over a German liner in the 1930s.

Below right: A Norddeutscher Lloyd advertisement from the early 1930s.

On the eve of the war, King George VI had just returned from a Canadian tour aboard the *Empress of Britain*. For her war service the *Empress of Britain* was pressed into service as a troopship. The Germans were well aware of this and made her a special target. In October 1940, in an area to the west of Ireland known to sailors as 'Torpedo Alley', the ship was caught by a patrolling German aircraft and disabled. The *Empress of Britain* was equipped with a very powerful radio installation and she managed to summon the assistance of a Polish destroyer and two tugs. Unfortunately the area was well named and before the ship could be towed to safety the passing *U32* fired two torpedoes into her. The *Empress of Britain* holds the dubious record of being the largest liner sunk in World War 2.

Shortly after the Japanese attack on Pearl Harbor on 7 December 1941, which brought the United States into World War 2, the *Normandie* (which had been interned in New York harbour) was taken over by the Americans. Originally the

right: The Italian liner *Rex*
(1932) sailed between
Genoa and New York from
1932 until 1940, taking the
Blue Riband in 1933.
From 1940 until 1943 she
was laid up because of the
war but was then taken over
by the Germans for use as a
troopship. *Rex* was
destroyed by aircraft of the
Royal Air Force in 1944,
south of Trieste.

Below right: The Italian
liner *Conte de Savoia*
(1932), like the *Rex*,
operated on the North
Atlantic until Italy joined
the Axis for World War 2.
Although Italy had
surrendered to the Allies on
8 September 1943, the
RAF still attacked and
destroyed the *Conte de
Savoia* on the 11th near
Malamocco in the
Mediterranean, fearing that
she would be used by the
Germans.

Below: The French liner
Champlain (1932), a one-
class vessel, sank after
striking a mine in 1940.

The New French Line steamer "CHAMPLAIN" Flagship of the One Class Cabin Fleet

Americans planned to convert the French
liner into an aircraft carrier but this idea was
soon abandoned in favour of using her as a
troop transport. Thousands upon
thousands of kapok life jackets were
brought aboard the ship and piled in her
grand salon while the conversion work
was going on. Shortly after 2.30pm on
9 February 1942 sparks from a welding
torch set fire to the life jackets. The
direct telephone link to the New York
Fire Department failed and before the
first fire engines reached the scene the
fire was well established. Thousands
of gallons of water were poured into
the ship in an effort to put out the
blaze. The liner slowly heeled over
because of the weight of water inside her
until, early in the morning of 10 February, she capsized at her
moorings. *Normandie* remained in that undignified situation for more than
18 months before she was finally righted and towed away to the breakers.

CANADIAN PACIFIC DUCHESS STEAMERS

Duchess of Atholl – Duchess of Bedford
Duchess of Richmond – Duchess of Cornwall

Above: Liverpool's
Gladstone Dock in the
1930s with Canadian
Pacific's *Duchess of
Bedford* and *Duchess of
Atholl* at the quayside.

Left: Cunard's
Mauretania[1] at
Southampton in the
early 1930s.

Right: The Pacific Steam Navigation vessel *Reina del Mar*, which operated between Liverpool and South America in the 1930s, 40s and 50s.

Below: Holland America's *Nieuw Amsterdam* (1938).

THE PACIFIC STEAM NAVIGATION COMPANY

s.s. REINA DEL MAR (20,225 tons)

Right: Colour card showing Holland America's *Nieuw Amsterdam* to good effect.

right: The French liner *De Grasse* (1938), which was taken over at Bordeaux by the Germans in 1940, and scuttled by them when the Allies liberated France. The *De Grasse* was raised and refitted by the French after the war and resumed her interrupted North Atlantic career before being sold off to Canadian Pacific in 1953. Canadian Pacific renamed the ship *Empress of Australia*[2] and it is in that incarnation she appears here.

below: The Dutch liner *Simon Bolivar*, while outward bound for the West Indies, sank in the North Sea after striking a mine on 18 November 1939.

EMPRESS OF AUSTRALIA 19,380 tons.

278

The War Illustrated

Yet Another Sea Crime in the Nazi Score

December 2nd, 1939

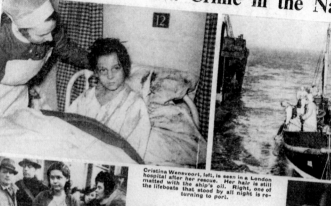

Cristina Wensvoort, left, is seen in a London hospital after her rescue. Her hair is still matted with the ship's oil. Right, one of the lifeboats that stood by all night is returning to port.

Those not needing treatment were taken to London hotels, outside one of which Joan Tresteill is standing.

THE sinking of the Dutch liner "Simon Bolivar" in the North Sea on November 18 with heavy loss of life, was described by the Admiralty as being "a further example of the total disregard of international law and the dictates of humanity shown by the present German Government." With astonishing effrontery and an almost insane belief in the credulity of neutral nations, the Nazis endeavoured to clear themselves of the guilt for this piratical crime by stating the ship must have been sunk by a British mine. That mines were strewn widely about the open seas by the Nazis is proved by the fact that by midday on November 20 it was announced that seven ships had been destroyed by mines and two others damaged.

At an East Coast port many pathetic scenes were observed. Here a survivor carries a small baby who has not been claimed.

Simon Bolivar," which was sunk 18 miles from the English coast by a German mine (probably laid by a submarine minelayer), was of 8,309 tons. She was outward bound from Holland to the West Indies and had on board about 400 persons, of whom 140 were at an East Coast port. Of the eighty British subjects among the passengers a number were included in the list of over a hundred missing.

In October 1942, during an eastbound crossing loaded with troops, the *Queen Mary* collided with an escort cruiser, HMS *Curacao*. The liner sliced the smaller ship into two, which quickly sank with the loss of 338 lives. Because of her precious cargo the *Queen Mary* did not stop, or even reduce speed.

Throughout the war both of the 'Queens' served as troopships and transported almost two million soldiers between them. Over a dozen other Cunard ships served as armed merchant cruisers. By the time the war ended in 1945 the Cunard line had lost nine vessels. The *Laconia*[2], *Lancastria*, *Laurentic*[2], *Carinthia*[2], *Bosnia* and *Andania*[2] had all been sunk, *Lancastria* with horrific loss of life. *Antonia* became HMS *Wayland*, *Aurania*[3] was HMS *Artifex* and *Alaunia*[2] had become HMS *Alaunia*.

After the war Cunard resumed its North Atlantic services. The *Queen Mary*, *Queen Elizabeth* and *Mauretania*[2] were refurbished and the *Ascania* was rebuilt. New cargo ships came into service, such as the *Asia*[2] and the *Arabia*[3]. Two new, first class only, liners became the line's first postwar passenger ships: *Media* and *Parthia*[2].

In 1947 Cunard bought up the last available shares in Cunard White Star Ltd from the Oceanic Steam Navigation Realisation Company, which had been formed solely to realise what assets had remained to OSN when it collapsed. The following year *Britannic* returned to the Southampton to New York run.

The new *Caronia*[2] entered service in 1949. She was comparable to the *Mauretania*[2] in size and speed but had been purposely built to work as a North Atlantic liner in the summer and as a cruise liner for the rest of the year. In a complete departure from normal practice the new ship was painted all in green instead of the usual black hull, white superstructure and red funnels. At the end of the year the Cunard Line took over all of the stock of Cunard White Star and the White Star part of the name was dropped. However, the *Georgic*[2] and the *Britannic*[3] continued to sail in White Star livery and under the famous red burgee with its white star above the Cunard house flag. The following year the old *Aquitania* was disposed of after 580 Atlantic crossings and 1.5 million passengers safely carried.

The *Samaria*[2] and *Ascania*[2] came into service with Cunard on the Canadian route in 1953 and 1954 to replace the ageing *Franconia*[2] and *Scythia*[2]. Between 1955 and 1957 the four largest Cunard steamers ever produced for the Canadian service were built: *Saxonia*[2], *Carinthia*[3], *Sylvania*[2] and *Ivernia*[2]. In 1956 the *Georgic*[2] went to the scrapyard. The last White Star liner, *Britannic*[3], left New York on 25 November 1960 for the final time to a salute from a Fire Department vessel, an honour usually reserved for ships completing their maiden voyages.

By the mid-1950s only two Canadian Pacific liners remained: the *Empress of England* and the *Empress of Canada*[3]. These saw a few more years' service but the *Empress of England* was sold off in 1970 and the *Empress of Canada* followed in 1972. It was the end of the road for the Canadian Pacific transatlantic liners. The final passenger ship belonging to the line, the *Princess Patricia*, was retired in 1982. By the late 1980s all of the company's passenger shipping interests were gone and all that remained were some cargo carriers which were operated by BCP Ship Management of London.

The Cunard White Star Superliner "QUEEN ELIZABETH" (On War Service)

Above: Cunard White Star's *Queen Elizabeth* in her wartime colours. A US Navy blimp scours the surrounding water for signs of any lurking German U-boats.

Left: Liverpool Prince's landing stage

Above right: The Cunard White Star liner *Queen Elizabeth* at sea

Right: The *Queen Elizabeth* entering New York harbour.

Cunard RMS "Queen Elizabeth"

By 1960 Cunard had 10 first-class passenger liners in th[e] Queen Elizabeth, Queen Mary, Mauretania[2], Caronia[2], Medi[a] Parthia and the four new ships on the Canadian route but the age [of] the liner was fast coming to an end. More and more passengers we[re] travelling by air because it was so much faster. Without th[e] passengers to fill them it was uneconomic to run the liners and the[y] began either to be sold off or converted into cruise ships. Media an[d] Parthia were sold and in 1963 Saxonia[2] and Ivernia[2] were refitte[d] for cruising and renamed Carmania[2] and Franconia[3] respectivel[y]. Although this left only six liners, that was still too many and they a[lso] served as cruise ships when the necessity arose. By 1965 it wa[s] apparent that the fleet would have to be reduced yet further and th[e] Mauretania[2] was sold for breaking up.

On 24 November 1966 Sylvania took the last Cunar[d] passenger sailing from Liverpool to New York. From this poi[nt] onwards what Cunard liners remained would operate out [of] Southampton only. In November 1967 the Queen Mary was sol[d], her days as an ocean liner over. She remains afloat as a conventi[on] centre at Long Beach, California. Early the next year the Quee[n] Elizabeth was also sold and was to suffer a similar, ignominious, fa[te] to that of her sister. After the failure of the initial plan, at Fo[rt] Lauderdale, Texas, she eventually found her way to Hong Kon[g] harbour where, while being converted into a floating university sh[ip] caught fire, burned out and sank. Much of the wreck remaine[d] above water and served as a tourist attraction.

Queen Elizabeth 2, the penultimate large liner built for Cunar[d] entered service in 1969 and joined the cruise ships Carmania[2] an[d] Franconia[3], all that remained of Cunard's once impressiv[e] passenger fleet. Even this situation could not last and in 1971 th[e] Carmania[2] and Franconia[3] were sold to the USSR, apparentl[y] leaving the Queen Elizabeth 2 as the last Cunard liner. Cunar[d], however, demonstrated its faith in the future of large passeng[er] ships, even if they are only cruise liners, with the introduction i[n] January 2004 of the new Queen Mary 2. It seems that liners are n[ot] quite ready to leave the world's stage.

Above: A Cunard White Star brochure advertising fares and sailing dates of the *Queen Elizabeth,* 1948.

Right: The Holland America Line's *Nieuw Amsterdam* in the 1950s.

Left: The American liner *America* (1940).

Below: The French liner *Lipari* on a 1940s transatlantic voyage.

S.S. "AMERICA" (33,532 GROSS TONS)

Left: The French liner *La Marseillaise.*

Above: The Holland America vessel *Ryndam* (1951) in the 1960s.

Left: By the 1950s Cunard had dropped the White Star part of its name, as can be seen in this advertisement.

Below: Holland America's *Maasdam* (1952) seen here a few years before being sold to the Polish Ocean Line and renamed *Stefan Batory*.

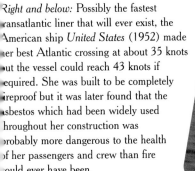

Right and below: Possibly the fastest transatlantic liner that will ever exist, the American ship *United States* (1952) made her best Atlantic crossing at about 35 knots but the vessel could reach 43 knots if required. She was built to be completely fireproof but it was later found that the asbestos which had been widely used throughout her construction was probably more dangerous to the health of her passengers and crew than fire could ever have been.

"UNITED STATES."

'S.S. United States."—Built by Newport News Shipping and Dry Dock Co., completed 20th June 1952. Length, 990 ft.; Breadth, 101½ ft.; Depth, 122 ft.; Weight, 53,330 tons; Speed, over 35 knots. Quadruple screw steam turbines. Holder of the Blue Riband for the fastest West/East and East/West Atlantic crossings.

Right: Empress of England, a Canadian Pacific liner launched in 1956, which served the company for 21 years.

Canadian Pacific

PASSENGER LIST

Programme for Today

Above: A 1956 passenger list from the Canadian Pacific liner *Empress of England*, which was leaving Montreal on 28 May 1965 bound for Liverpool via Greenock.

Above right and right: *Queen Mary's* programme of passenger entertainment for 31 August 1959.

NOTICES

U.S. LANDING CARDS AND CUSTOMS DECLARATION FORMS

Passengers who have not yet collected their U.S. Landing Cards and Customs Declaration Forms from the Purser's Office, " A " Deck, are requested to do so today

Please Present Passports, Vaccination Certificates and Travel Documents when making application.

Only one member of a family need attend.

CREW EMERGENCY EXERCISE

At 11.00 a.m. today the Alarm Gongs will be sounded throughout the ship. This is an Emergency Exercise for the crew only and does not affect Passengers in any way

COMPETITION WINNERS

Superlative Quiz—MRS. J. MAYS

Passenger List (1)—MRS. R. BULLOCK

Group Competition—MR. B. JOYNSON CORK

BRIDGE, CHESS OR CANASTA

It is suggested that passengers wishing to meet others who are interested in playing Bridge, Chess or Canasta should meet in the Smoke Room (Promenade Deck) at 2.30 p.m. today.

CLOCKS

Clocks will be STOPPED for ONE HOUR at Midnight

FIRST CLASS

R.M.S. "QUEEN MARY"   Monday, August 31, 1959

PROGRAMME OF EVENTS

a.m.

7.00-2.00 p.m.—5.00-7.00 p.m.—Swimming Pool available (weather permitting)   "R" Deck

          Sun Deck

7.00-7.00 p.m.—Gymnasium open for exercise

Passenger List Competition (2)   Gymnasium

8.15-10.00—Keep-Fit Class (Gentlemen)   Gymnasium

11.00-Noon—Keep-Fit Class (Ladies)   Prom. Deck Square

11.15—Daily Run "Tote" (closes 11.50 a.m.)   Main Lounge

11.30-12.30—Robin Simpson at the Hammond Organ   Main Lounge

p.m.

2.30—Recorded Music   Main Lounge
          Symphony in C Major, " The Great " (Schubert)
          The Halle Orchestra. Conductor : Sir John Barbirolli

3.45—Melody Hour   Main Lounge
          Robin Simpson at the Hammond Organ

4.00—Children's Tea Party   Restaurant

4.30—Movie: "BLIND DATE"   Cinema
          Featuring Hardy Kruger, Stanley Baker and Micheline Presle

6.15—News Broadcast (British)   Long Gallery

6.30—News Broadcast (American)   Long Gallery

7.30—Cocktail Hour   Observation Lounge

From 7.30—GALA DINNER   Restaurant

7.30-8.15—Cocktail Dancing   Long Gallery
          " Queen Mary " Dance Orchestra, conducted by Harry Taylor

8.15-9.30—Strolling Minstrels   Restaurant

9.15-9.45—Orchestral Selections   Main Lounge
          "Queen Mary" String Orchestra, directed by Clarence Myerscough

9.30—Movie: " BLIND DATE "   Cinema
          Featuring Hardy Kruger, Stanley Baker and Micheline Presle

9.45—HORSE RACES   Main Lounge
          Interludes at the Hammond Organ

9.45-10.30—DANCING   Long Gallery
          " Queen Mary " Dance Orchestra, conducted by Harry Taylor

10.45—DANCING   Main Lounge
          " Queen Mary " Dance Orchestra, conducted by Harry Taylor

DANCING will continue from approximately 12.30 a.m. in the Starlight Roof Club (Verandah Grill). No cover charge

Left: The Holland America Line's *Rotterdam* (1959), the flagship of its fleet.

Below: Canadian Pacific's *Empress of Canada*[3] (1960), which remained with the line for only 12 years before being sold as a cruise ship.

Above: Cunard's *Carinthia*[3].

Right: Canadian Pacific liner *Empress of Britain*[3], launched by Her Majesty Queen Elizabeth II in 1955.

Left: The flagship of the Canadian Pacific fleet. *Empress of Scotland* in the 1950s. Originally named *Empress of Japan* (1929), she sailed between Liverpool, Southampton and Quebec for the first 10 years of her life. Between 1939 and 1948 she worked as a troopship, being renamed in 1942 (for obvious reasons) the *Empress of Scotland*. From 1950 until 1958 she returned to transatlantic service but was then sold off to the German Hamburg Atlantic Line and renamed *Hanseatic*. She finally went to the breakers in 1966.

Right: A 1960s card showing the 'Queens of the Seas'. By this time the great days of the transatlantic liners were over.

Below: Passengers on A Deck of Canadian Pacific's *Empress of Canada*[2] in the early 1950s.

Bottom: Cunard's *Franconia*[3] which was built in 1954 as *Ivernia*[2] but renamed in 1962.

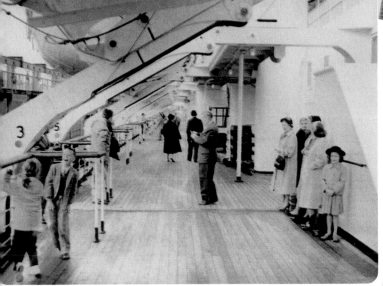

Above: Notepaper from Cunard's *Ivernia*[2] (1954). The ship was sold to Russia in 1971.

Cunard R.M.S. "Sylvania"
AT THE LANDING STAGE, LIVERPOOL.

S.S. SAXONIA, CUNARD LINE
21,637 GROSS TONS.   LENGTH 608 FT.   BEAM 80 FT.   SPEED 20 KNOTS.

PRINTED IN ENGLAND

Left: Cunard liner *Sylvania*[2], sister ship to *Ivernia*[2] and *Saxonia*[2].

Far left centre: Saxonia[2] berthed at a Liverpool landing stage.

Far left bottom: Saxonia[2] sailing up the River Mersey.

Below left and right: Cunard's *Queen Elizabeth 2* (1967): more a cruise ship than a transatlantic liner.

Below: The old world meets the new. *Queen Elizabeth 2* berthed at *Titanic's* old moorings while the Red Rover coach and four stands in the foreground.

Red Rover Coach and Four and Queen Elizabeth 2 at Southampton. E1BH

Menu cover from *Queen Mary*, August 1959.

INDEX

erdeen & Commonwealth Line 84	Austrian 20, 36	Caronia 31, 34, 39, 63, 65	Dickens, Charles 13
yssinia 17	Baltic 14, 17, 38	Caronia² 1, 65, 114, 116	Dominion (Line) 18, 31, 34, 38, 78
adia 13	Baltic² 17, 32, 33, 34, 96	Carpathia 31, 57	Donaldson Line 15, 53
riatic 14, 17, 72	Bardic 72	Carthaginian 19, 30	Doric 34
riatic² 37, 43, 96	Bartlett, Captain 14	Castilian 22, 23	Doric² 78, 96, 07, 103
ric 26	Bavarian 23, 30, 36	Cedric 43, 53, 72, 96	Duchess of Atholl 111
aska 18	Beaver Line 23	Celtic 17, 34	Duchess of Bedford 86, 111
aunia² 113	Belgic 18	Celtic² 53	Duchess of Richmond 87
aunia, HMS 113	Belgic⁴ 72	Champlain 109	East India Company 12, 13
bania² 72	Belgeuland 72	Charles Bartlett 14	Elder Dempster 29, 34
bany 38	Bellona 31	Charlotte Dundas 11	Ellerman (Line) 31
berta 38	Berengaria 78, 94	China 17	Emden 63
bertic 96	Berlin 72	Christian Huygins 96	Empress of Asia 63, 66
ecto 15	Bethania 64	Circassian 19, 20, 21	Empress of Australia 113
geria 17	Binns, Jack 37-8	City Line 34	Empress of Britain 64, 66, 97, 102, 103, 108
lan (Line) 11, 14, 18, 19, 20, 22, 23, 26, 30, 31, 34, 38, 39, 47, 52, 53, 54, 57, 59, 67	Bismarck 7, 37, 78	City of Bombay 34	Empress of Britain³ 122
ps 14	Black Star Line 16	City of Brussels 15	Empress of Canada 87
satian 53, 61, 69	Blue Riband 14, 15, 16, 18, 20, 37, 96, 97	City of Glasgow 14, 15	Empress of Canada² 123
mazon 14	Booth, A. (Cunard Chairman) 8, 9	City of New York 19, 20, 22	Empress of Canada³ 114, 121
merica 14, 116	Bosnia 113	City of Paris 15, 20, 22	Empress of China 20
merican 34	Bothnia 17	City of Philadelphia 14	Empress of China² 72
merican Line 18, 22, 23, 31, 78	Brazilian 20, 47	City of Vienna 34	Empress of England 114, 119, 120
nchor Line 15, 16, 18, 31, 47	Bremen 96, 100	Clan Line 96	Empress of France 58, 59, 62, 63, 71, 72, 75
dania² 72, 78, 113	Briarwood 97	Clermont 11	Empress of France² 86, 87
des 14	Britannia 12, 13	Collins (Line) 13, 14	Empress of India 20
atonia² 72, 78, 113	Britannic 18, 34, 70	Collins, Edward Knight 14	Empress of Ireland 36, 53, 58
quitania 2, 37, 53, 54, 61, 63, 71, 77, 78, 99, 114	Britannic² 37, 49, 51, 70	Colonian 72	Empress of Japan 20, 63, 122
abia 14	Britannic³ 9, 96, 104, 106, 107, 113	Columbia 13	Empress of Russia 63
abia² 113	British & American Steam Navigation Co 11	Columbus 34, 72	Empress of Russia² 72
abic 18	British & North Atlantic (Line) 31	Commonwealth 34	Empress of Scotland 72, 122
abic² 29, 34, 69	Brunel, Isambard Kingdom 10, 11, 15, 16, 22	Conte de Savoia 109	Etruria 5, 19, 20
abic³ 72, 96	Brunel, Marc 11	Coptic 18	Europa 14, 100
aguaya 83	Burns, George 13	Corean 19, 21	European 34
rctic 13, 14	Caledonia 13, 16	Corinthian² 23, 69	Fitch, John 10
rizona 18	Calgarian 53, 69, 71	Corinthic 31, 96	Florida 37, 38
rmenian 34, 69	Calgaric 96	Corsican 39	Formigny 103
rtifex, HMS 113	Californian 22, 30	Cretic 34, 72	France 52
scania² 72, 113, 114	Cambria 13	Crimean War 11, 17	Franconia 47
sia² 113	Campania 8, 20, 22	Cufic² 34, 96	Franconia² 72, 80, 114
siatic 17, 18	Canada 14	Cunard 1, 2, 5, 7, 8, 9, 11, 12, 13, 14, 16, 17, 18, 19, 20, 22, 23, 28, 30, 31, 37, 39, 40, 41, 42, 44, 47, 48, 54, 57, 63, 64, 69, 70, 71, 76, 77, 78, 79, 80, 81, 96, 97, 98, 99, 104, 105, 106, 107, 111, 113, 114, 115, 116, 118, 122, 123, 124	Franconia³ 116, 123
ssyrian 20	Canadian 19		French Line 18, 31, 32, 52, 53, 74, 97, 100
ssyrian Monarch 20	Canadian Pacific 8, 11, 14, 18, 20, 27, 34, 36, 47, 53, 60, 61, 62, 63, 66, 67, 70, 71, 72, 75, 76, 86, 97, 102, 103, 110, 111, 113, 114, 119, 120, 121, 122, 123	Cunard, Abraham 11, 12	Fulton, Robert 11
sturias 101	Canberra 18	Cunard, Samuel 11, 12, 13, 15, 17	Furness Withy Line 17, 30
thenic 31	Canopic 34, 72	Curacao, HMS 113	Gaelic 18
tlantic 14, 17, 18	Cap Trafalgar 66, 68	Cymric 60	Gallia 23
tlantic Transport (Line) 31, 34	Carinthia 22, 30	Damara 30	Gallic 72, 96
urania 19, 31	Carinthia² 72, 97, 113	De Grasse 113	Georgic² 96, 106, 107, 114
urania² 72, 97	Carinthia³ 114, 122	de Jouffroy d'Abbans, Claude François 10	Germanic 18, 34
urania³ 113	Carmania 31, 63, 64, 66, 68	Delphic 71, 96	Gigantic 37
usonia² 72, 78	Carmania² 116	Desna 53	Grampian 69
ustralasian 30			Great Britain 12, 13

Great Eastern 15, 16, 17, 19, 22
Great Western 10, 11, 13
Great Western Railway Co 11
Great Western Steamship Company 11, 13
Grecian Monarch 20
Gresham 38
Griscom, Clement 34
Guion Line 16, 18
Hamburg America (see also Hamburg
  Amerika) 7, 11, 18, 31, 37, 66, 78
Hanoverian 19
Hanseatic 122
Harland & Wolff 17, 18, 19, 23, 34,
  72, 78, 84
Harland, Edward 16, 17
Hawke, HMS 47
Hibernia 13
Hibernian 19
Highflyer, HMS 64, 66
Himalaya, HMS 63
Holland America (Line) 47, 70, 112, 116
Holliday, Charles 14
Homeric 72, 82, 96, 97
Hull, Jonathan 10
Huronian 31
Île de France 98, 100
International Mercantile Marine (IMM)
  8, 29, 31, 34, 72, 78
Imperator 37, 78
Inman 11, 18, 20
Inman, William 14, 15, 19, 22
Ionian 30
Ionic 31
Ismay, Joseph Bruce 9, 18, 23, 34, 106
Ismay, Thomas Henry 17, 18, 23
Ivernia[1] 1, 23
Ivernia[2] 114, 116, 123, 124
Java 17
Justicia 70
Kafiristan 97
Kaiser Wilhelm II 30
Kaiser Wilhelm der Grosse 22, 64
Kidston, William 13
Kronprinzessin Cecilie 33
Kylsant, Lord 9, 72, 78, 84, 86, 96
Laconia 47
Laconia[2] 72, 78, 113
Lake Champlain 8, 29
Lapland 53, 72
La Savoic 32
La Touraine 32
La Provence 53
La Marseilleise 117
Lancastria 72, 78, 113
Laurentian 21, 30, 47
Laurentic 38, 45, 46, 70
Laurentic[2] 84, 96, 106, 113
Leviathan 78, 82
Leyland (Line) 18, 31, 34, 72
Liberté 100
Lipan 117
Livonian 22, 70
Lucania 22
Luce, Captain 14
Lucerne 19

Ludgate Hill 22
Lusitania 29, 31, 37, 40, 42, 44, 52,
  63, 67, 68
Maasdam 118
MacIver, David 13
Magnetic 29, 32
Majestic 19, 20, 53, 78, 85
Majestic[2] 7, 82, 86, 96, 97
Manitoban 23
Marburn 27
Mauretania 31, 37, 41, 42, 78, 96, 111
Mauretania[2] 106, 113, 114, 116
Mayflower 34
Media 113, 116
Megantic 38, 46, 96
Melita 72
Melville, James 13
Metagama 61, 72
Minnedosa 61, 72
Minnewaska 34
Monarch Line 20
Mongolian 21, 30, 70
Montcalm 72, 75, 102
Montclare 72, 75
Monte Videan 20
Monterey 34
Montlaurier 72
Montrose 45, 72, 76
Montroyal 64, 66, 72
Morgan, John Pierpont 8, 29,
  30, 31, 34, 72
Napier, Robert 13, 17
New England 34
Newcomen, Thomas 10
Niagara 14
Nieuw Amsterdam 112, 116
Norddeutscher Lloyd (Line)
  (see also North German Lloyd) 11, 18,
  20, 21, 22, 30, 31, 64, 72, 96, 100, 108
Normandie 97, 104, 105, 108, 109
North Atlantic Ice Patrol 51
Northland 53
Norwegian 19, 21
Nova Scotia 21
Numidian 70
O L Hallenbeck 47
Oceanic 16, 17
Oceanic[2] 17, 22, 23, 53
Oceanic Steam Navigation Company
  (OSN) 17, 18, 84, 106, 113
Olympic 37, 47, 48, 51, 72, 74, 84, 96, 97
Ontarian 23
Ontarian 53
Orbita 83
Orcadian 23, 53
Oregon 18
Ormiston 23
Ottawa 34
P & O (Line) 18
Pacific 14
Pacific Steam Navigation Co 83, 112
Paris 74
Parisian 19, 20, 21, 23, 53
Parthia[2] 113, 116
Pennsylvania Steamship Co 14

Persia 9, 14
Persia[2] 16
Peruvian 36
Phillips, Owen 72
Phoenician 19, 20, 36
Pidduck, Henry 14
Pirrie, Lord 72, 78
Poland 78
Polynesian 19, 20, 21
Pomeranian 20, 22, 30
Pretorian 23
Princess Alice 21
Princess Irene 20
Princess Patricia 114
Pyrosaphe 10
Queen Elizabeth 7, 106, 107, 113, 114,
  115, 116
Queen Elizabeth 2 116, 124
Queen Mary 96, 105, 106, 107, 113,
  116, 120, 126
Queen Mary 2 9, 116
Rattler 15
Red Star (Line) 18, 24-5, 31, 53, 72, 78
Regina 71, 78
Reina del Mar 112
Republic 17, 37, 38
Republic[2] 34
Rex 109
Ribble, HMS 61
Richardson Line 14
Richmond Hill 22
Romanic 34, 47
Rosarian 20
Rotterdam 121
Roumanian 22
Royal Mail 11, 17, 72, 84, 96, 100
Royal Mail Steam Packet Co 11, 50,
  52, 53, 83
Royal George 70
Royal William 12
Royden, Thomas 17
Ruapehu 30
Runic 96
Russia 17
Ryndam 118
Samaria 17
Samaria[2] 72, 77, 97, 114
Sardinian 19, 20, 21, 30
Sarmation 19, 20
Savery, Thomas 10
Saxonia 23, 28
Saxonia[2] 114, 116, 124
Scandinavian 47, 69
Schwabe, Gustave 17
Scotia 16, 17
Scotian 47, 67
Scythia 17
Scythia[2] 72, 76, 114
Sealby, Captain William Inman 38
Servia 18
Shaw Savill Line 19, 31, 84
Siberia 17
Siberian 19, 21, 30
Sicilian 23, 30, 67
Simon Bolivar 113

Sirius 11, 1
Southland 53, 7
Sphinx 8
St Louis 2
St Michael 7
St Paul 2
State Line 21, 2
State of Alabama 2
State of California 21, 2
State of Georgia 2
State of Indiana 2
State of Nebraska 2
State of Pennsylvania 2
Statendam 4
Stefan Batory 11
Sydney, HMAS 6
Sylvania 114, 116, 12
Symington, William 1
Tainui 2
Teutonic 19, 20, 22, 5
Thames 3
Titanic 9, 22, 31, 37, 48, 51, 53, 54, 55
  56, 57, 12
Tower Hill 2
Tropic 17, 1
Tropic[2] 34, 9
Tunisian 23, 26, 27, 6
Turanian 2
Twin Screw Line 1
Tyrrhenia 7
U24 6
U32 10
U54 7
U99 10
UB64 7
UB124 7
Ultonia 2
Ulunda 3
Umbria 19, 2
Unicorn 1
United States 11
Vaderland 5
Vaterland 78, 8
Vedic 72, 7
Verne, Jules 1
Victorian 34, 37, 3
Vindictive, HMS 7
Virginian 37, 38, 53, 55, 6
Voigt, Johann 1
Waldensian 2
Watt, James 10, 1
Wayland, HMS 11
White Oak 1
White Star 5, 8, 9, 11, 16, 17, 18, 19, 20
  22, 23, 26, 29, 31, 32, 33, 34, 37, 38, 43
  45, 46, 47, 48, 49, 53, 69, 70, 71, 72, 78
  2, 83, 84, 85, 86, 96, 97, 101, 104, 106
  107, 108, 114, 118
Williams, Captain James Agnew 1
Wilson Line 20
Wilson, President Woodrow 72
Worcester, Marquis of 1
Zeeland 53
Zeelandic 38